It's My Turn

It's My Turn

Ruth Bell Graham

World Wide
A ministry of the Billy Graham Association

1303 Hennepin Avenue
Minneapolis, Minnesota 55403

Unless otherwise identified, Scripture quotations are from the King James Version of the Bible.

Scripture quotations identified RSV are from the Revised Standard Version of the Bible, copyrighted 1946, 1952, © 1971 and 1973.

Scripture quotation from the Amplified New Testament, © The Lockman Foundation 1954, 1958.

E. H. Hamilton's poem "Afraid? Of What?" is used by permission of the author.

Quotation from "The Road Not Taken" from THE POETRY OF ROBERT FROST edited by Edward Connery Lathem. Copyright 1916, © 1969 by Holt, Rinehart and Winston. Copyright 1944 by Robert Frost. Reprinted by permission of Holt, Rinehart and Winston, Publishers.

Several poems are from *Sitting by My Laughing Fire* by Ruth Bell Graham, copyright © 1977 by Ruth Bell Graham; used by permission of Word Books, Publisher, Waco, Texas 76796.

Quotation from *The Holy Bible* (From Ancient Eastern Manuscripts) translated by George M. Lasma © 1957 Holman Bible Publishers. All rights reserved. Used by permission.

Library of Congress Cataloging in Publication Data
Graham, Ruth Bell.
  It's my turn.
    1. Meditations   2. Graham, Ruth Bell.
  I. Title
BV4832.2G64   242   82-5387
ISBN 0-8007-1274-9   AACR2

This edition is published by special permission from the original publisher, Fleming H. Revell Co., Old Tappan, NJ.

For
YOU

Contents

You have heard from one who has had a generous portion of the earth for his parish. You are about to hear from one who had their home and their five children for hers.

The size of the parish is immaterial. But the message and the goals have been essentially the same.

Having sometimes heard speakers whom I should have liked to shut up and put on a shelf, I have chosen to write so that a busy person can shut me up and put me on a shelf when they have had enough.

This volume is primarily a sampling of experiences from what, for me, has been a full and interesting life. Some are implanted vividly in my memory today. Others are collected from old journals, letters, and an assortment of notebooks.

Not all of them are autobiographical, for I have learned much from others. But I have learned the most from an old, eternally contemporary Book and its Author.

Again, if these experiences are a mixture, that's life.

I shall be telling this with a sigh
Somewhere ages and ages hence:
Two roads diverged in a wood, and I —
I took the one less traveled by,
And that has made all the difference.

ROBERT FROST

Evening was creeping along the valleys and up the ridges. The breeze rustling leaves in the treetops had stilled. Not even the chatter of a katydid broke the silence.

I was rocking quietly on the front porch when our six-year-old burst through the screen door, letting it slam behind him. He settled noisily into the rocker next to mine and whispered, "Shhh. Be quiet, Mom. Don't make any noise ... and you will hear plenty of nuffin."

So we shushed, were quiet, didn't make any noise, and heard plenty of nothing.

Finally I whispered, "Do you like hearing nothing?"

"No," he replied. "I like noise!"

With that, he bounded out of the rocker and jerked open the screen door. Darting inside, he let it slam behind him.

Me? I like "plenty of nothin'." It's the noise of civilization that disturbs and grates. Nature's noises, I have discovered, refresh and relax me.

The rustle of the wind in the tops of the trees or the roar of it across the ridge behind the house...

The chirping of a cricket or the orchestration of katydids from mid-summer until frost...

The full moon rising, huge and silent, over Little Rainbow Ridge.

The expectant stillness...

On such evenings, Bill and I will sit together on the front porch when he is home, quietly talking, or, when words are not needed, just listening to "plenty of nothin'."

And along with the deepening shadows in the valleys below, the darting of the evening's first bat across the darkening sky, come the memories...

"Lord, Thou art Life tho' I be dead,
    Love's Fire Thou art, however cold I be:
Nor heaven have I, nor place to lay my head,
    Nor home, but Thee."

                CHRISTINA ROSSETTI

The thirteen-year-old girl lay in the stifling heat of the old missionary home at Number Four Quinsan Gardens, in the port city of Shanghai, China, praying earnestly that she would die before morning.

Dawn broke over the great, gray city, and obviously, God had not seen fit to answer my prayer.

It was September 2, 1933, and time for me to start high school. The school our parents had selected was the Pyeng Yang Foreign School in what is today Pyongyang, North Korea.

My older sister, Rosa, had been there the preceding year. Rosa, eager to try her wings, was a good adjuster and had taken it all in stride, enjoying it thoroughly.

I was leaving all that was loved and familiar to me: the Chinese friends, the missionaries, home; Daddy, Mother, and thirteen years of treasured memories.

So with Mother, Daddy, and our former tutor, Miss Lucy Fletcher, to see us off, five of us missionary children boarded the Nagasaki Maru, berthed in the Whangpoo River, and moved slowly through the muddy waters to where the even muddier waters of the mighty Yangtze River emptied into the East China Sea. The journey took us the better part of a week. Finally we arrived in Pyeng Yang.

I do not remember how we were transported to the school. It doesn't really matter now. I only remember the sense of finality as we progressed through the surprisingly wide streets, passing modern buildings interspersed with ancient Korean ones, until we entered a narrow, tree-lined lane, made our way up the hill, and were deposited in front of the girls' gray brick dormitory.

Once we had been assigned to our Spartan dormitory room, the homesickness settled in unmercifully. The days I could manage. It was the nights that did me in. Burying my head in my pillow, I tried not to disturb my sleeping roommates, Rosa and Helen Meyers. Night after night, week after week, I cried myself to sleep, silently—miserably.

Sick in the infirmary for a few days during this period, I propped myself on my pillows and spent an entire day reading the Psalms — all 150 of them. The tiny corner room in that small infirmary building remains a warm glow in my memory because of the strengthening from those timeless, timely passages.

How could I know this was my training period—my boot camp? Preparation for my future.

Recently I was watching a television program which showed marines training at boot camp. It was tough, it was rough, it was dangerous. And yet how much tougher, rougher, and more dangerous real combat would be were it not for this basic training?

Looking back over my life, now I can see the importance of those difficult times at Pyeng Yang and I am grateful.

And grateful, also, for my roots.

Ruth Bell in 1933, just before leaving for school in Korea.

Giants

There were giants in the earth
in those days...
                    Genesis 6:4

 Miss Edith Spurling ran the old, very British missionary home in Shanghai, China. Miss Spurling was also old and very British.

She once commented that she looked forward to the Southern Presbyterian missionaries' arrival: they had such good times together.

They did. I was fortunate to have grown up among them. Happy Christians are a part of my heritage.

And those I knew were deeply committed to Christ.

One would have to be to go to China in those days, learn the difficult tonal language, and work as hard as they did, often under dangerous circumstances.

For example, an oil company, about to open a new operation in China, had a committee meet in an all-night session. The object was to find a man to manage the new division. This manager had to meet four qualifications: he had to be under thirty years of age, a university graduate, a proven leader, and have a fluent working knowledge of Chinese. Each man considered was found lacking.

Then someone said he knew a man meeting all the requirements who already was living in China, in the very city where the company was planning to establish headquarters. He was twenty-eight years old, had a brilliant college record, had three years' study and practice in the Chinese language, plus the full confidence of the Chinese people among whom he was well known.

When someone asked how much salary this young man was getting, the committee was startled to learn that it was only six hundred dollars a year.

"There must be something wrong!" exclaimed the chairman.

"There is," replied the man. "But it's not with my friend; it's with the system that employs him. He works for a mission board."

After further questioning, the chairman appointed his friend to go to China with the instructions, "Hire that man. Offer him ten thousand dollars a year. If that fails, offer him twelve thousand dollars or even fifteen thousand dollars."

The agent made the long trip, found his friend, and made him the offer, which was declined. As instructed, the agent raised the offer, but was again refused.

Finally the agent asked, "What will you take?"

"It's not a question of salary," the young missionary assured him. "The salary is tremendous. The trouble is with the job. The job is too little. I feel that God has called me to preach the Gospel of Christ. I should be a fool to quit preaching in order to sell oil."*

Such were the giants among whom we grew up.

---

*This story is told in *Tales From the Middle Kingdom* by A. F. and G. C. Willis.

Speaking of giants, when Daddy and Mother landed in Shanghai in 1916 (Daddy, fresh out of the Medical College of Virginia in Richmond, and twenty-two years old), Mother was a slim 114 pounds. "Poor little Virginia Bell!" one missionary is reported to have exclaimed. "She won't last a year!"

She fooled them. She not only lasted a year—she lasted twenty-five of them before returning to the States to live another thirty-three.

She built a house, had three children, buried one, had two more, taught her children at home through the fifth grade, ran the women's clinic, always had another missionary or two in the home, planned the menus, taught the cook how to prepare American food, checked accounts with him daily, examined each piece of linen as it came back from the hospital laundry to make sure no bedbugs were hiding in the folds, entertained often and well, and wrote home faithfully.

In the evenings she saw to it that we played games together or that we "womenfolk" did handwork (knitting, embroidery, braiding rugs, crocheting, and sewing) while the men took turns reading aloud books ranging from Dickens, *Uncle Remus, Ben Hur,* to Sir Walter Scott. Evenings were family times for us.

Daddy was the head of the surgical work in the hospital. Dr. James B. Woods directed the medical work. They believed the hospital existed primarily for the preaching of the Gospel. A full-time evangelist was employed to minister to the men patients, and a Bible woman to the women. Gospel tracts were given not only to the patients but to the families, who, according to local custom, accompanied them to the hospital.

This did not mean that Daddy and Dr. Woods did not run a tight ship. They developed a hospital that the American Medical Association eventually recognized as qualified for the training of interns from this country. And on his fortieth birthday, Daddy was made a Fellow of the American College of Surgeons.

Daddy was a man's man: an athlete, a daredevil, a practical jokester. He loved music, played the guitar, and had a fine singing voice. He laughed heartily and found much to laugh over. He was also known as a hard worker, moving quickly and surely through life as if he always knew where he was going and what God would have him do.

And I'm sure he did, for I cannot recall getting up in the morning but what Daddy would be reading his Bible (and his greeting, "Ruth, have you read your Bible yet?" frequently sent me back to my room to begin the day as I should), or on his knees getting his instructions from God.

Those instructions were always practical and down-to-earth, which is, after all, where Daddy lived.

The following incident illustrates just how very down-to-earth he could be.

One night we were driving through the narrow streets of Tsingkiang, approximately 250 miles north of Shanghai, in Kiangsu Province.

It was summertime and the isinglass flaps which served as windows in the little British Austin were off.

Progress through the narrow, stone-paved streets was slow and precarious because it was both sidewalk and street, and packed with people. Along with the occasional ricksha, and the barrow men carefully balancing their heavily loaded wheelbarrows, trotted the bucket bearers, carrying pungent night soil balanced at each end of the *biendan* across their shoulders. Occasionally, the car had to come to a full stop while some merchant pulled his wares back into his shop in order to make room for us to pass.

It was at a point when the car had come almost to a standstill that a young boy, peering in along with scores of other Chinese to see the "foreign devils," took full advantage of the situation and let loose with a well-aimed mouthful of spit. The car moved just slightly and, missing Daddy, it landed *splat!* right on me.

Daddy slammed on the brakes and bolted out the door. The culprit, sensing disaster, took off through the crowd as fast as his legs could carry him. But Daddy, in his earlier days purchased as a pitcher by the Baltimore Orioles, was no mean athlete himself, and while the little boy had size on his side, Daddy had determination on his.

Back through the narrow streets they tore, the crowd parting to let them pass, some people startled, others amused, realizing, no doubt, that the "foreign devil" had good reason for what he was doing.

Through the eastern gate of the mud wall they went, up onto the narrow-gauge railroad track (on which I never saw a train), and down the tracks, until finally Daddy overtook the culprit, turned him over his knee, and spanked him soundly.

What a man!

Dr. and Mrs. L. Nelson Bell and family in China.

China was in turmoil, as it had been off and on for more than four thousand years. The revolution of 1911 had overthrown the increasingly corrupt Manchu regime that had ruled China since 1644.

Various foreign countries had sought to carve out a piece of China for their own interests during the previous century, creating much bitterness and deep resentment. Disputes, fighting, and mini-wars were commonplace. There were conflicts among warlords, bandits, the Japanese, Communists, and Nationalists. When an uprising would turn anti-foreign, the various consuls would advise those under their jurisdiction to leave temporarily. The average Chinese person was unable or unwilling to distinguish between those foreigners who went to China to exploit her and those who went to serve her. All foreigners were "foreign devils."

Some missionaries knew what it was to be looted a number of times. It is a great way to learn how unimportant "things" are.

Even such occasions can have their humorous aspect. On returning to Taichow from one such "forced vacation," Uncle Kerr Taylor and Uncle Pete Richardson were told by the gateman that it had not really been necessary for the missionaries to leave.

"Why, we were told we would have been killed if we had stayed here!" one missionary exclaimed.

"Oh, you would have been killed the first two or three days," the old gateman replied, adding reassuringly, "but after that you would have been all right."

Gunshots broke the stillness of the countryside — gunshots and the occasional barking of dogs.

It was bandit country. Yet Daddy and Mother never showed fear; and their attitude somehow rubbed off on us.

Treating gunshot wounds was a daily occurrence in the hospital. We once asked Daddy what was the largest number of gunshot wounds at any one time.

"Over six hundred," he replied, adding, "after the battle of Taierchuang."

We children vividly recall one rather grisly story Daddy was known to tell on occasion. The local soldiers had captured two bandits. One of them had a serious head wound. While on a visit to the jail on Sunday morning, Daddy patched him up with compassion and skill, leaving his wounds cleansed, neatly stitched, and carefully bandaged.

Three hours later, Daddy was asked to make a house call inside the ancient city walls. As he drove under the massive east gate, he looked up, and there, hanging over the gate, was this same head — bandages and all.

When living in an area where, and at a time when, kidnapping for ransom was not uncommon, what did one do? Wealth is comparative, but to the Chinese bandit of that day, the average foreigner appeared wealthy.

Our Mission Board made it a policy *never to pay ransom*. That policy spread rapidly by word of mouth. As a result, none of our missionaries was ever held for ransom.

Uncle Jack Vinson,* however, was captured and killed by bandits, in cold blood.

Uncle Jack was recovering from an appendectomy when the village of Yangchiagih (a village in which a number of Christians lived) was pillaged by bandits. Uncle Jack insisted on going to check on the Christians. While he was there, the bandits returned. Uncle Jack was captured, and after being roped together with a long line of prisoners, was ordered to start walking. Because of his recent surgery, he was unable to keep up. A bandit threatened to shoot him if he did not hurry.

A young Chinese girl heard the threats and Uncle Jack's reply: "If you shoot me, I shall go straight to heaven." The soldier shot him.

When Uncle Ham (the Reverend E. H. Hamilton) heard the account of the shooting, he wrote the following poem which reflects, I think, the feelings of all those missionaries under whose influence we grew up.

---

*To the children of missionaries, most fellow missionaries were "aunt," "uncle," or "cousin."

Afraid? Of What?

Afraid? Of What?
To feel the spirit's glad release?
To pass from pain to perfect peace,
The strife and strain of life to cease?
    Afraid—of that?

Afraid? Of What?
Afraid to see the Savior's face
To hear His welcome, and to trace
The glory gleam from wounds of grace?
    Afraid—of that?

Afraid? Of What?
A flash, a crash, a pierced heart;
Darkness, light, O Heaven's art!
A wound of His a counterpart!
    Afraid—of that?

Afraid? Of What?
To enter into Heaven's rest,
And yet to serve the Master blest,
From service good to service best?
    Afraid—of that?

Afraid? Of What?
To do by death what life could not—
Baptize with blood a stony plot,
Till souls shall blossom from the spot?
    Afraid—of that?

E. H. HAMILTON

Mr. Kao Er was a jolly, cheerful man. He was the business manager of the hospital as well as the younger brother of the local pastor.

One night while Mr. Kao Er was attending prayer meeting at the hospital, bandits broke into his house and carried off his eight-year-old son and baby daughter. Word spread quickly. Many heads were shaken in sympathy. The missionaries and Chinese Christians gathered and prayed.

Then Mr. Kao Er, never one to miss an opportunity to witness for Christ, had a large sign painted and posted at the congested street crossing in front of the hospital gate. It said, in effect: "The bandits have kidnapped our children and demanded a thousand yuan in ransom. I am not a wealthy man. I cannot pay one thousand yuan ransom. I cannot pay five hundred yuan. I cannot even pay fifty yuan. But I believe God. If it is His will, He is able to bring my children back without any ransom."

The headshaking continued, along with laughter and ridicule. Get a kidnap victim back, without ransom? Only in a coffin! And if ransom was not paid promptly, as likely as not the family would receive a severed finger of the victim to hurry up ransom payments. If these were not forthcoming, perhaps an ear would follow.

But for the kidnap victim to be returned without ransom being paid was unheard of. So while the unbelievers shook their heads, the Christians bowed theirs.

Long weeks passed. The soldiers and the bandits clashed again in the north countryside, and the bandits were routed. In hot pursuit, the soldiers heard a sound from the ditch beside the road. Curious, one stopped to look, and found a skeletonlike child lying in the ditch where the bandits had, in their hurry to escape, thrown him. Too weak to walk, he was carried to a tea shop in the nearby town.

A soldier sat him on a bench where he could lean against a wall. A cup of tea was set before him, but his clawlike hands shook so, someone had to hold it to his lips.

"What is your name?" he was asked.

"And your father's?"

"Mr. Kao Er," the boy replied, and told them where his father worked and what had happened. The reason for his weakness was that his captors had imprisoned him under a large inverted gong (an earthen vessel used to contain fermenting pickles or, as we used it, for water). A crowd gathered.

That very day, a male nurse from the hospital had gone home to the village for a visit. Seeing the crowd of people, he joined them, craning his neck to see what the attraction was. What he saw and heard was "the unheard of": a kidnap victim free in answer to prayer. After identifying himself, the nurse hired a ricksha, lifted the boy onto it, and carried him back to his father in triumph.

News of the boy's return spread rapidly and was met by amazement on all sides. Even the Christians were astounded. I remember that we children prayed together by ourselves, and I remember how excited—and surprised—we were that God had answered.

But what about the baby girl? She had just recovered from the measles at the time of her capture. And moreover, she was still nursing. Even though "the unheard of" had happened in regard to the boy, generally it was agreed that the baby girl could not possibly have survived. And the head-shaking (though itself a bit "shook up") and the praying (now reinforced) continued.

Later, there was another battle between the bandits and the soldiers. This time, among those captured was the wife of the bandit chief. Oddly, she was nursing two babies — not twins, yet too near in age to both be her own.

Under questioning, the woman admitted that the older baby had been kidnapped from the home of the business manager of the foreign hospital in Tsingkiang. As a result, the little girl was returned safely to her parents.

Sitting one Sunday in the little gray brick Chinese church, I watched as Mr. Kao Er, carrying his still-too-weak-to-walk son, and his wife, carrying the now healthy, chubby baby girl, walked forward to publicly give thanks to God for doing "the unheard of," and to dedicate both children to Him.

The tall missionary walking down the narrow, crowded village street overheard two gentlemen sitting in a tea shop exclaim in Chinese, "Here comes the *Yang Kuei-tse* [foreign devil]!"

Chinese tea shops opened directly onto the street, and as the missionary came parallel to it, he paused. Then, sitting down at the same table with the two gentlemen, he greeted them pleasantly in Chinese.

Surprised, they returned his greeting, then asked with customary Chinese courtesy, "What is your honorable surname?"

"Yang," replied the missionary with a straight face.

"And what is your honorable first name?"

"Kuei-tse," replied the missionary, his eyes twinkling.

Suddenly comprehending the humor of the situation, the three threw back their heads and roared with laughter.

We grew up feeling she was a large, reliable, kind, and understanding Rock of Gibraltar. Then one day we put her on the scales. She was a reliable, kind, and understanding Rock of Gibraltar, but as for being large, even in her padded winter garments she barely weighed ninety-six pounds.

"She's a homely old soul," Mother once commented, arousing in us an indignant response. Then we looked at her more objectively. Her nose was unusually broad and flat, and there was a mole on one side of it. Her eyes were little more than slits with short, very straight eyelashes framed by laugh wrinkles. Her mouth was wide and kind. A peasant's face. A pleasant peasant face. Mother was right. She was a homely old soul, and yet so kind and loving a character we children would have sworn she was beautiful.

She was our *amah* as we grew up: our Chinese nurse, Wang Nai Nai. And we children were not the only ones who loved her. Everyone did. And with good reason: she loved everyone.

I can still see her sitting on a low stool in the upstairs back bedroom, her paper hand-bound Chinese hymnal open in her hands, singing in her plain, flatly nasal voice the Chinese words to Cowper's famous old hymn:

> "There is a fountain filled with blood
> Drawn from Immanuel's veins,
> And sinners plunged beneath that flood
> Lose all their guilty stains.

"The dying thief rejoiced to see
That fountain in his day,
And there may I, though vile as he,
Wash all my sins away."

And to my innocent child's mind, she was the picture of a saintly old soul at worship. Not until years later, when we were considered "old enough to be told about such things," did we learn how perfectly Cowper's old hymn fit Wang Nai Nai.

For when much younger, Wang Nai Nai and her husband had been "procurers." That was a time when baby girls were not generally wanted. So the shady business of buying unwanted girls to sell to certain houses in Shanghai was not difficult.

But one day, Wang Nai Nai heard from Aunt Sophie Graham, one of the pioneer Presbyterian missionaries, about a God who loved her but hated sin. To become a child of God one must repent of sin and ask God for forgiveness through His Son, Jesus.

It was as blunt and simple as that.

Wang Nai Nai repented and turned to God.

Mother and Daddy told how when she first came to work for them, she longed to be able to read her Chinese Bible for herself. They found her flat on the floor one night, close to the fireplace with her Bible open, trying to learn the charactrs by the light of the dying fire. After that, they bought her a lamp of her own, as we had no electricity then. And so she taught herself to read the Bible.

Of such material God makes some of His choicest saints.

The old Book lies on a shelf high above my desk, encased in a frayed, slip-on leather cover, its own cover long since dislocated, the pages loose, dog-eared, and heavily marked. It is the same old treasured Bible I carried with me when I went to high school in North Korea.

I had studied it carefully in all my Bible courses, had read it for daily guidance and comfort, and it was to this same old Book I had turned in desperation those first early days of my homesickness in high school at Pyeng Yang.

It was here I stumbled across that verse, "When my father and my mother forsake me, then the Lord will take me up" (Psalms 27:10). It never once crossed my mind that I had been deliberately forsaken. I knew that after being taught by Mother for as long as she could handle it, and then having been tutored for three years by a superb teacher whom several missionary parents had secured at their own expense to teach us children, our parents had reached the conclusion that there was no alternative now but to send us off to the best school they could locate.

That I had been "forsaken" was, to my childish way of thinking, obvious but necessary. It was typical of Daddy and Mother that they selected the school they considered the best — not the one nearest home. That's why we went to North Korea.

I had, as it were, cut my teeth on the Bible, and do not recall a time when I did not love it. So it was to the Bible that I turned for comfort during the months of homesickness in North Korea.

That first Fall at Pyeng Yang Foreign School (PYFS for short), I had what some might call a "crisis of faith," although that sounds a bit grand for a thirteen-year-old's first doubts. Still, age has nothing to do with a crisis, and the subject was my faith. Perhaps it resulted from unanswered prayer. I had begged God (and my parents) to let me go home: without success.

Or it may have been spiritual growing pains.

Like the young man who went to a delightfully sane bishop to confess he had lost his faith.

"Nonsense," replied the bishop. "You've lost your parents' faith. Now go out and get one of your own."

I knew God had sent His Son, Jesus, to die for the sins of mankind, but somehow I did not feel included. There were so many and I was only one, and, let's face it, not a very significant one at that. I prayed for forgiveness and felt nothing. I wasn't even sure He was listening.

Finally, in desperation, I went to my ever-practical sister, Rosa, and asked her advice.

"I don't know what to tell you to do," she replied matter-of-factly, "unless you take some verse and put your own name in. See if that helps."

So I picked up my Bible and turned to Isaiah 53, one of my favorite chapters. I did just what she suggested—I read, "He was wounded for [Ruth's] transgressions, He was bruised for [Ruth's] iniquities: the chastisement of [Ruth's] peace was upon Him; and with His stripes [Ruth] is healed" (*see* verse 5).

I knew then that I was included.

Shanghai fell to the Japanese on August 13, 1937. It was a brutal victory. The bombs that fell indiscriminately on the city left thousands of civilians dead or wounded.

The day before I was to have left home for Shanghai to board the ship for the United States and college, the Japanese mined the Yangtze River and blew up the Nanking-Shanghai railway. The missionaries in our station were urged by the consul to head north to Haichow, where the United States Navy would have a destroyer pick us up.

It was a difficult but interesting trip. I had been geared to an earlier departure, so each succeeding day was like a reprieve—a stay of execution. There were the few remaining days at home where, all preparations and packing for college completed, Mother and I relaxed and enjoyed life.

Then the boat by canal to Haichow, where an American destroyer picked us up and deposited us in the port city of Tsingtao. There were the happy days with the family in a beach house in Tsingtao.

Daddy was finally able to secure a berth for me on a troopship evacuating naval families from the war zone to Japan and the United States. Again there were good-byes. I boarded with Betty McLaughlin as a traveling companion. Betty, slightly older, had been visiting her family and was returning to college and her fiancé. She was looking forward, I was looking back.

I was older now and more mature, so leaving this time was not the traumatic experience that the first departure from Shanghai had been.

In Japan we left the *Chaumont* and boarded the S.S. *President McKinley*, packed with navy dependents being returned to the States. Our quarters in steerage were just in front of the propellers, which caused a constant vibration. The walls of our stateroom were the thick metal hull of the ship. Four elderly missionary ladies shared the room with us.

There were two suicides that trip. The radio in the States commented, "The S.S. *President McKinley* announces the loss of two passengers at sea."

Needless to say, our families breathed a sigh of relief when they learned we had safely arrived in the States.

Wheaton is a liberal arts college near Chicago. Like our school in Pyeng Yang, Korea, it had a warm Christian atmosphere. I felt as if I had come home as soon as I arrived on campus.

One's spiritual survival and growth is not necessarily dependent upon one's roots, or the environment within which one grows. Some strong Christians have started life like the babies of the ancient Spartans, who were left exposed overnight to see if they were able to survive, and therefore fit to live. Others have been nutured lovingly and with care. Daddy and Mother were of the strong opinion that life is a battleground and that homelife and schooling should be a training ground. I was a child of such thinking.

The atmosphere at Wheaton was not hostile to my still-simple, childlike faith. It was like a home away from home. Looking back over the years I spent there, I'll have to admit that I learned more from people than I did from books. Except for my major (which was Bible) and art (which was my minor), the textbooks and classroom discussions made little impression on me. The primary influences in my life came from people — classmates, roommates, friends, teachers, members of the community.

An indifferent scholar, I have wondered why the proverb "Wherefore is there a price in the hand of a fool to get wisdom, seeing he hath no heart to it?" (Proverbs 17:16) was not hung in large letters on the wall where students went to pay their bills. At the same time, I soaked up impressions like a sponge. And here again, as in my childhood and later on in high school in Korea, the people who influenced me the most exemplified kindness.

A sensitive nature makes one vulnerable to hurts. A person does not have to be deliberately hurt to feel pain. Thoughtlessness, sarcasm, tone of voice, indifference—each has the ability to wound. Each time something unpleasant happened to me, there was the subconscious decision never, if possible, to hurt someone else that same way. For me, therefore, it became a valuable bit of training.

On one occasion I inadvertently broke a college rule and was rebuked so harshly I felt completely demolished. At the same time, my sister Rosa happened to be in the school infirmary recovering from a bout with pleurisy. Going to her room, I buried my head on the side of the bed and dissolved into tears.

On the other hand, the now famous Dr. Edman left his mark on me, as he did on thousands of other Wheaton students, by his kindness and gentle affirmation.

There is a good reason God has told us to "be kind to one another" (*see* Ephesians 4:32).

And then there was my naiveté. Growing up in China made me worldly-wise in many ways, but incredibly naive in others.

"What did you have for Thanksgiving dinner in China?" my dinner companion, Harold Lindsell, asked that first Thanksgiving at Wheaton College. "Did you have turkey?"

"No," I replied, "we ate bastards."

Looking a bit startled, he exclaimed, "I doubt that!"

"Yes," I insisted, "we had one every Thanksgiving. They were quite good."

Still looking skeptical, he said, "I think not."

Upset by his attitude, I exclaimed indignantly, "I ought to know. I've eaten plenty of them!" Whereupon he changed the subject.

Later, while visiting my sister Rosa, who was still sick in the infirmary, I was telling about my lunch with Harold Lindsell and the strange dinner conversation, wondering why he had taken exception to what I had said. Rosa thought it was hilarious.

"What's so funny?" I asked.

"Oh, you nut!" she exclaimed. "They weren't bastards. They were bustards. They were wild geese called bustards."

The Coat

One semester, Elizabeth Walker, a close friend, and I decided that we would give up the privilege of eating in the upper dining hall and move to the lower dining hall in order to give the difference in cost to a student we knew on campus who was in real need.

The upper dining hall was cafeteria style. One ate at small tables, and the atmosphere was decidedly more pleasant. The lower dining hall was in the basement of Williston Hall, one of the girls' dormitories, and one ate family style at long tables. The difference per semester wasn't all that much. But there was a need and we felt this was an opportunity to help, so we took it.

Later I saw the student whom we were anonymously helping, wearing a coat which even I could not afford.

My instant reaction was indignation. Then it was as if the Lord Himself asked, *Are you doing this for her—or for Me?*

I had to admit that basically we were doing it because we loved Him.

That's all I wanted to know, He said.

It was all I needed to know. She could have worn sable and it would have made no difference.

When I wrote home about the incident, Daddy's cryptic response was typical of his clear thinking and direct approach to problems. While it might have been a nice idea, he admitted, he was paying my way through college, and it really was not my money to juggle as I pleased.

I learned two good lessons from one experience.

And Cain went out from the presence of
the Lord, and dwelt in the land of Nod....
Genesis 4:16

 While never even remotely a scholar, the horror of
failing drove me to try.

Among some old college papers I found the following sched-
ule (for how long it lasted I do not recall). It indicates I
occasionally made a stab at studies.

3:00 - 4:00 A.M.	Devotions
4:00 - 5:00	
5:00 - 6:00	Greek
6:00 - 7:00	
7:00 - 8:00	Dress and go to school
8:00 - 9:00	Greek
9:00 - 10:00	Lit
10:00 - 10:30	Chapel
10:30 - 11:30	Study history
11:30 - 12:30	History test
12:30 - 1:30	Archery
1:30 - 2:30	Study Bible
2:30 - 3:30	Bible class
3:30 - 4:30	Tower picture
4:30 - 5:30	Art lab
5:30 - 6:30	Supper
6:30 - 7:30	Special feature
7:30 - 8:30	
8:30 - 9:30	Greek
9:30 - 10:30	I have house prayer meeting

Two years of Greek was required for a Bible major. The phrase "It's Greek to me" suddenly made sense. Greek itself certainly didn't.

During the "Greek Period" I found myself burning the proverbial candle at both ends. I was late to bed and up at 3:00 A.M. That gave me time to begin the day with Bible reading and prayer, then struggle with a strange alphabet and an even stranger vocabulary.

The only place I could study without disturbing my sleeping roommates was in the bathroom. Here I was able to sit, propping my feet on the end of the tub and using my knees for a desk.

One morning the alarm had awakened me—but not quite. I was reading in Genesis. Heavy-eyed, I struggled through history's first murder, when the jealous Cain killed his brother, Abel.

Suddenly I awoke with a start. I had fallen asleep, my head resting heavily on the Bible. Blinking my eyes to get them focused, I located where I had left off: Genesis 4:16. The next verse had me awake and laughing. It read, "And Cain went out from the presence of the Lord, and dwelt in the land of Nod . . . ."

"Ruth," said an old high school friend who had been studying at a secular university, "you ought to lose your faith. It would do you good."

No one had ever suggested that to me before, and it took me completely by surprise. But the seed was planted and it began to bear fruit, slowly but relentlessly.

I cannot say that I became an atheist. It takes more faith to be an atheist than to believe in God. It was impossible for me to look at the heavens at night without realizing there had to be a Creator. But I could not be sure the Bible was God's message to man, and if I could not be sure of that, I could not be sure that Jesus was who He claimed to be.

I began to argue. I argued with anyone who was willing to argue. It got to where friends would avoid me, knowing confrontation was inevitable.

"Here comes Ruth," was the general opinion of my friends, "we're in for another argument."

They didn't understand: I wasn't arguing to win, I was arguing desperately to lose. I wanted them to come up with valid reasons that I was wrong and they were right.

At that time, I had been dating a senior reputed to be one of the most brilliant students on campus. It didn't take him long to realize my predicament.

"You're having problems with your faith, aren't you?" he asked one day.

"You can say that again!" I replied. "Let's go and see so-and-so," he suggested, naming a deeply spiritual professor on campus.

I objected.

"He will talk with me, and pray with me, and it could even get a little emotional. I don't want that. All I want are cold, hard facts." I wanted to go see Dr. Gordon Clark, known for his logic, his unemotional brilliance. I felt he would give me nothing but the cold, hard facts.

My friend wound up by explaining to me simply, factually, and logically why we believe the Bible is God's message to man, whom He had made—man, who had turned his back on God, for whom God felt responsible, and to whom God was reaching out.

I do not remember all the arguments. Today they seem unimportant. What I do remember is the final step. At the very end he said, "There is still the leap of faith." It was exactly what I needed: the clear, terse arguments, the merciless logic, and finally, the "leap of faith."

If God could be reached only through intellect, then where would the brain-damaged, the mentally retarded, the little child be? When Jesus put the little child in the midst of His disciples, He did not tell the little child to become like His disciples; He told the disciples to become like the little child. And some of the greatest intellects of the ages— Saint Augustine, Blaise Pascal, G. K. Chesterton, C. S. Lewis, and countless others—have all had to come the same way, in simple, childlike faith.

How like God!

His aging face was rugged and deeply lined, this head of Wheaton's Bible department. He may not have been the best of teachers, Dr. H. C. Thiessen, but he was one of the godliest and kindest. My mind frequently wandered as he taught us from the textbook on Bible doctrine which he himself had written. But when he came to the part about God's Son giving His life to redeem us sinful mortals, the strong voice never broke, but the tears would begin to trickle down those worn seams — as if they had done it before, as if perhaps they had sort of worn those grooves there in the first place.

Occasionally, he would wipe them away with the back of his hand, as if unaware of doing so, as one, deeply concerned about something important, might brush away a fly.

It was another illustration to me of the fact that true scholarship and deep love for God frequently go hand in hand.

And then there was Miss Edith Torrey, daughter of the scholarly evangelist Dr. Reuben Archer Torrey.

How would you like to be taught Bible by Miss Betsey Trotwood, straight out of Dickens's *David Copperfield?* Miss Torrey was tall, angular, bony, and bespectacled. She taught the Bible with a thoroughness that frightened you. But behind that austere countenance was a heart of gold.

I owe her a debt of gratitude not only for the sound Bible instruction which I received in her classes but also for the surprising fact that she prayed Bill and me together.

After we were safely and surely engaged, she told us that she had been praying for months that this would happen. Years later, after she died, her niece, Betsy Parker Shank, while going through her belongings, came across her old Bible, in which she kept a prayer list. Included in this list were the grammatical errors my husband made while preaching on radio's "Hour of Decision" during those early days. Knowing how I would enjoy them, Betsy sent the copy to me.

Daily chapel attendance was a requirement for all Wheaton students. It was the highlight of the day for me. We sat in alphabetically assigned seats, and were rotated every few weeks. My last name being Bell, at one time I found myself on the front row, right under the speaker's nose.

I owned two pairs of shoes then, one for dress and a pair of brown and white saddle shoes for school. These had been handmade in Tsingtao before I left China and were my pride and joy. Each night I polished them carefully. One snowy day, during the message, I happened to glance down. The snow on my shoes had melted and with it the white shoe polish. There I sat, my feet planted firmly in a slowly expanding white puddle. I kept my eyes intently on the speaker, hoping everyone else was doing the same.

If we did not have a stirring missionary speaker, some well-known Bible teacher, or evangelist, we had one of the college professors. My favorite all-round speaker was Dr. V. Raymond Edman, history professor, who later became the president of the college. He was always brief (a nice quality) but right on target.

Since childhood I had felt a strong tug toward serving God as a missionary in Tibet. It could have been a pipe dream, as Bill dreamed, as a boy, of growing up to play big-league baseball. "Dreams are like stars," someone has said. "You do not touch them with your fingers, but you steer your course by them." Or, it could have been God checking out my willingness.

No doubt the exposure to missionary speakers in these chapel services reemphasized the mystique of this inaccessible land and led me to the conclusion that I was called to minister there. And I planned to go alone.

God had another idea.

All I saw was a blur. I was on the steps of East Blanchard when a new student passed me. I was going up. He was going down.

He's surely in a hurry, I thought to myself, and went on.

Sunday mornings we had a prayer meeting in Williston lobby before dividing up and going out on gospel team assignments. That morning I heard a new voice pray: strong, clear, urgent.

There is a man who knows to Whom he is speaking, I thought.

I had heard about this new transfer student, who had come from a Bible college in Florida. They said he was a gifted preacher—a young man on whose shoulder God's hand seemed to rest.

Shortly after that, a friend, Johnny Streater, introduced us. Not long after, Bill asked me for our first date—a Sunday-afternoon presentation of *The Messiah.*

Now one does not get to know a person by sitting and listening to a group singing, however inspiring the music. Yet that night I knew he was the one. Someone has said, "Feminine instinct is a great time-saver: it enables a woman to jump at conclusions without bothering with the facts." So I laid it before the Lord and left it there.

Still there was Tibet.

Gently, tactfully, persistently, I tried to suggest and then to persuade Bill that perhaps he, too, should go to Tibet as a missionary. It was obvious that I was doing the calling, not God. Weeks passed.

Finally Bill turned to me: "Do you believe that God brought us together?"

I did — unquestionably.

"In that case," Bill said firmly, "God will lead me and you will do the following."

And I have been following ever since.

Looking back, if I had insisted on having my way, I would have lasted in Tibet four years at the longest. Then that part of the world closed to foreign missionaries. And I would have missed the opportunity of a lifetime of serving God with the finest man I know, having five terrific children, and fifteen of the most delightful, interesting, and lovable grandchildren imaginable. All this, plus an unusual if not easy life.

I believe God had a part in my desire to go to Tibet. I think He was testing my willingness while at the same time *preparing* me for many long separations.

Mine has been the task of staying home and raising the family. No higher calling could have been given me. At the same time, it has been loads of fun. Also, I've had a vicarious thrill out of my husband's travels around the world in his unceasing attempt to carry the Good News to all who will listen.

If I had not longed to go to Tibet at one time, I might have been tempted to feel sorry for myself. As it is, I feel I have had the best of both worlds: being able to stay home with the children and also being able to keep up with Bill through the press, by phone, and by mail; and, on occasion, traveling with him.

"Where two people agree on everything,
one of them is unnecessary."

A group of ladies from the "Tab," where Bill was student minister, gave me a shower shortly before we were married. Each of them wrote a bit of advice on a piece of paper and gave it to me. The above quote was the pick of the lot.

How often that saying came to mind and how necessary I felt!

I have met wives who did not dare to disagree with their husbands. I have met wives who were not permitted to disagree with their husbands. In each case, the husband suffered. Either he became insufferably conceited, made unwise judgments, tended to run roughshod over other people, or was just generally off-balance. However, it is a good thing to know how to disagree and when.

Here are a few suggestions out of my own experience: First, define the issue (and make sure it is worth disagreeing over); next, watch your tone of voice and be courteous (don't interrupt, and avoid rude, unkind, or unnecessarily personal remarks); third, stick to the subject; fourth, stick to facts; and fifth, concede graciously.

As for when to have a disagreement, this takes both sensitivity and ingenuity on the part of the wife as well as the husband.

For one thing, it is not wise to disagree with a man when he is tired, hungry, worried, ill, preoccupied, or pressured.

(That doesn't leave me many opportunities.)

Nor does it pay to argue with your husband unless you are looking your very best. The woman who argues with her hair in rollers has ten strikes against her to begin with.

And avoid arguing when you are boiling mad over some issue. Sleep on it first, if possible, then try to discuss it calmly and objectively. Likely as not, by then you won't be able to remember what you were upset about in the first place.

A Christian wife's responsibility balances delicately between knowing when to submit and when to outwit. Adapting to our husbands never implies the annihilation of our creativity, rather the blossoming of it.

It was our first major disagreement after our marriage. Home for us was the second story of a house about a block from the Burlington Railway in Hinsdale, Illinois.

Some of Bill's bachelor friends had come to visit. One day they decided to drive to Chicago for the day.

I asked if I could please go along. I wouldn't bother them. I'd just window-shop (all I could afford to do), and meet them at some appointed time for the trip back.

"No," said Bill. "We guys just want to be alone. No women today."

No amount of pleading moved him. Taking the only car (I didn't know how to drive then, anyway), they headed for the city. Through my tears I watched the car swim out of sight. The walls of the dreary little apartment began closing in. Even the bit of bright-red satin Chinese embroidery I had hung on the wall, with a desk lamp shining on it to give the illusion of a glowing hearth, failed to bring warmth and cheer.

Kneeling beside the overstuffed chair, tears pouring furiously down my face, I prayed, "Lord, if You'll forgive me for marrying him, I'll never do it again."

Undoubtedly the dumbest prayer I ever prayed.

Later, Bill realized how thoughtless he had been and apologized profusely. Young husbands seldom mean to be cruel, but being new at the business of marriage, and unable to see things the way new brides do, they can be thoughtless.

But as Robert Quillen said, "A happy marriage is the union of two good forgivers."

And after the forgiving comes laughter, a deeper love — and further opportunities to forgive!

Long, long ago, in the prehistoric days of our marriage, we were having a not-unusual difference of opinion. Now I come from a long line of strong-minded people — strong-minded and outspoken.

I don't think the men in Bill's family were accustomed to strong-minded and outspoken women. So there were Times.

This was one of them.

"I have never taken your advice before," Bill told me bluntly that dumb, dark day, "and I don't intend to begin now."

"I'd be ashamed to admit," I replied rather disrespectfully, "that I had married a woman whose advice I couldn't take."

And that was that.

Sidetracked?

Twice Bill got sidetracked from his calling as an evangelist — or so it seemed to me at the time.

The first was when he accepted a church pastorate.

The second time was when he accepted the presidency of a college.

In neither case was I consulted. Which doesn't mean I didn't express my opinion.

In looking back, I can see God's purpose in both. In his two years as pastor, Bill came to understand the problems of pastors, so that in the years that have followed, wherever he has gone to hold crusades, he knows that without the cooperation and help of the local pastors, such meetings would be impossible. The local pastors also are the ones to take over and shepherd the new Christians after the crusade has left. They are the farmers, as it were, while Bill and those with him are the itinerant reapers.

The experience at the college was similar. It gave him an understanding and appreciation for educators and a love for students that he might not have had without this experience.

I cannot say these were the mistakes I thought they were at the time. Even if they were, God is able to take those mistakes, when they are committed to Him, and make of them something for our good and for His glory.

Usually the most difficult part of any marriage will come in the first few months or years. This will probably be due largely to differences in background, personalities, and the unavoidable tensions of marriage.

My side of the family had been Presbyterians for generations.

Mother and Daddy went to China under the Southern Presbyterian Mission Board. I recall joining our little Chinese Presbyterian church when I was eleven. My membership stayed there until Bill and I settled in Montreat in 1944 and I had my letter transferred here. And these are the only two churches I have ever belonged to.

Loyalty was deep in my makeup, and the more the Baptists tried to make a Baptist out of me, the more the old Bell stubbornness rose to the surface. I prayed and I studied, while the Baptists began putting the heat on Bill for having a "disobedient wife."

The time came when Bill invited a leading Southern Baptist minister to breakfast with us in order to set me straight.

I explained my position simply. In Montreat, a Southern Presbyterian conference center, we have only one church — a Southern Presbyterian church. If I could not get to church for some reason (a sick child or a new baby in the family), Daddy and Mother (who had returned to reside permanently in the United States in 1941) took the children to church for me. If I drove to the neighboring town of Black Mountain to attend the Baptist church, who would take the children when I couldn't go with them? Furthermore, they would become confused.

I wanted more than anything else for the children to grow up, not so much aware of denominational differences, but aware of the reality of the Lord Jesus Christ Himself.

This particular pastor, an immensely kind man, listened without interruption. I concluded by saying that when the children were grown, they would be free to decide for themselves what denomination they would like to join.

At this point our friend leaned forward. "But Ruth," he inquired very earnestly, "have you ever considered that" ... pause ... "that they might *choose to remain Presbyterians?*"

As it has turned out, they are a mixture: Lutheran, Baptist, Christian and Missionary Alliance, Presbyterian, and Plymouth Brethren. It is the person of the Lord Jesus Himself who is all-important to each one—that, and the preacher's faithfulness to God's Word. Not the denomination.

I remember one time during those stormy days when I was being pressured to switch denominations. We were on a visit to Florida. I was sitting on the beach late at night after Bill was asleep, tears streaming down my face.

"Why the emphasis on denominations?" I asked the Lord. "Isn't Jesus Himself the issue?"

Jesus Himself *is* the issue. Our Baptist friends eventually began to realize that I belonged to Him, if not to them. And our differences in background have proven to be an asset in the ministry which God has given Bill, rather than a detriment, for the message of Redemption is above denominationalism.

Bill's and my tastes differ (in books, music, style, decor, food, hobbies, and so forth). Even our forms of relaxation differ. I go for a good book. He, immersed in books most of the time as it is, used to play golf, now runs two miles a day. Grateful for the excuse of an arthritic hip, I can walk but not run.

Our temperaments differ. By nature I am easygoing to the point of laziness, and am basically optimistic. Bill is highly disciplined and drives himself unmercifully. The family affectionately refers to Bill as "Puddleglum"—a modern-day Jeremiah.

"Puddleglum," for those of you who have not been introduced to this delightful individual, appears in one of C. S. Lewis's children's stories, *The Silver Chair*. He is the extraordinary character known as a Marshwiggle, who joins Eustace and Jill after they are sent by Aslan to find Prince Rilian. (If you are getting confused, go buy the book. It's worth it.)

Puddleglum has the boundless capacity for seeing the grim side of every situation. Each simple statement or dire prediction is either preceded or followed by, "I shouldn't wonder." In the end he turns out to be the most sterling character in the entire book, true-blue to the core.

The classic case of my Puddleglum's "I shouldn't wonder" attitude came once when we landed at the Miami airport. Bill had to stay, while I was to fly home. He checked the weather and learned it was not good in Atlanta, Georgia, where I would have to change planes for Asheville, North Carolina.

"You probably won't be able to land," he predicted. "If not, I don't know where you will go—probably on to New York City. But if they try to land, I hope you make it; Atlanta is one of the busiest airports in the United States. And if you do, I'd advise you to spend the night in a motel—if you can get a room, which I doubt—as a lot of planes will be grounded and the motels will be full. In that case, rent a car, if you can get one, and drive home. But drive carefully because..."

You guessed it. "...you could have a wreck!"

Still laughing as I climbed aboard the plane, I pulled out my notebook to jot down this choice bit of "I-shouldn't-wonder" before I forgot it. Incidentally, the plane landed safely, I transferred with no trouble, and the plane to Asheville made it without difficulty. But this was The Classic, the statement we as a family have enjoyed to the fullest, the one which even Bill had a good laugh over when I read it back to him.

At the same time, let me say that there is no one—but no one—who is better in an emergency than Bill. He remains calm while his mind races like a jet airplane, and he is capable of making correct decisions quickly and decisively.

We had just moved into our newly remodeled home on the corner lot across the road from Daddy and Mother's corner lot in Montreat, North Carolina.

We had purchased the Parks' old summer cottage because of its location and the fact that the generous lot had a number of large oak trees, a little stream running between the yard and the road, and on both sides of the stream a heavy growth of rhododendron bushes.

Borrowing what we could, we remodeled. It turned out to be unique. We furnished it with leftovers done over, junkyard discoveries, and homemade lamps. (Bill used to say you could always tell which lamp I had made because when he turned it on, it went off.) But what it lacked in furnishings, it did make up in charm.

While I was in the hospital having Anne, our second daughter, Bill decided there was no point in owning such an attractive little house if our neighbors couldn't even see it. He gave instructions for all the rhododendron bushes along the road to be cut, so as to share the house with the neighborhood.

Fortunately, the workmen knew how much store I set by the trees on the place, particularly the protective wall of rhododendron.

Unfortunately, one man (instead of pretending to have misplaced his ax) blurted to Bill, "Mebbe we ought to wait till Mrs. Graham gets back."

Bill did not like this one bit, but wisely, he bided his time.

Anne and I were warmly welcomed home from the hospital. What could be more blissful than coming into a newly remodeled home with a new baby, and watching her being lovingly welcomed by father, older sister, and grandparents!

Later, it surfaced.

Coming from a man who loves his privacy, I was surprised by the instructions in the first place. But by then, so was Bill. He came to appreciate those rhododendron bushes as much as I did.

It was the fact of not having his order followed on his own property that challenged his sense of being head of the house.

Since he was in agreement about the bushes by that time anyway, things settled happily into their routine.

Only once more, after the initial encounter over the rhododendron hedge, did Bill seriously complain about his apparent lack of authority around the place. I cannot remember the exact circumstances, only the complaint that his authority seemed to end at home.

It was then that I asked him if he would like me to come to him whenever the furnace needed fixing, the house needed repainting, the cesspool needed to be cleaned, or repairs needed to be made.

I was more than willing to bring these things to his attention, but knowing the enormous load he carried—the continual preparation of sermons as well as the running of a growing organization, a daily newspaper column, and a book usually in the process of being written, besides an endless pile of correspondence—I hadn't the heart to bother him with these details.

It was then, I think, that he began to see the sensibleness of the setup. Proverbs 31 substantiates this division of labor. A woman assumes the household responsibilities to free her husband for his.

Remodeling the old summer cottage, which was later furnished with leftovers, junkyard discoveries, and home-made lamps.

Preoccupied

My husband is frequently preoccupied. Understandably. He has a lot to be preoccupied about.

We were expecting company for dinner, and I asked him what he would like to have on the menu.

"Uh-huh," he grunted. I knew he was with me in body only, and decided to have some fun.

"I thought we'd start off with tadpole soup," I began.

"Uh-huh."

"And there is some lovely poison ivy growing in the next cove which would make a delightful salad."

"Uh-huh."

"For the main dish, I could try roasting some of those wharf rats we've been seeing around the smokehouse lately, and serve them with boiled crabgrass and baked birdseed."

"Uh-huh."

"And for dessert we could have a mud soufflé and . . . ." My voice trailed off as his eyes began to focus.

"What was that you said about wharf rats?" he asked.

"Billy, there's a little cove I'd like to show you," Mike Wiley said to Bill one day. "It belongs to a couple of mountain families, but I think you could buy it reasonably."

"Let's go," Bill said. "We'll take my car."

"Won't make it," Mike objected. "Road's too narrow. Get in my Jeep."

That's how we first saw it. The road was incredibly narrow, winding, and steep. Old Man Solomon Morris had originally built it, using first a mule and a plow, followed by a mule and a drag pan. Eventually, a mule could make it up with a wagon. And a Jeep could make it. The rhododendron bushes crowded in on both sides.

After what seemed a long time, we passed a modest shack on our left, covered with tar paper, windows and doors filled with staring, unsmiling faces. The right side of the narrow road dropped almost vertically to the tiny stream-bed below. Evidence of a harvested corn crop in this unlikely spot gave a clue as to how the family supplemented its meager income.

As we rounded the next curve, we had to slow down to ford the same streamlet that passed through a tiny valley on our left, crossed the dirt road, and dropped on down the mountain. Around the next bend beneath a cluster of large, freshly topped white pines on the outcropping of the hogback above, and a small pole cabin to our right, we reached the end of the road.

The two mountain families and two old bachelors had scraped a living off these acres mainly by harvesting the larger trees for lumber, so that all that was left were the culled ones.

The number of gallon jars confirmed our idea of how else they supplemented the harvesting of trees. I have real sympathy for mountain families living out cold winters in unheated cabins. They just might need some antifreeze.

Not having garbage collection, whenever they finished with something, they simply pitched it down the mountain. It was all pretty sorry looking, but it was a generous chunk of land and the price was reasonable — somewhere between twelve and fourteen dollars an acre.

Finally Bill said, "I'll leave it up to you, Ruth. While I'm in California, you decide."

It was isolated, it was loaded with possibilities, and I loved it. So while he was in California, I borrowed the money from the bank and bought it.

When Bill returned, I told him.

"You *what?*" he exclaimed.

Abe had worked for our friend's family for years. He was an elderly black man with a high sense of loyalty and a fine sense of ethics. After his retirement, he was allowed to charge his groceries to the family whom he had served so long and so well. He took advantage of this generous provision but was scrupulously careful in allowing no member of his family to presume on it.

When our friend was preparing to get married, old Abe called on him.

"I want to give you a bit of advice," he said, settling himself comfortably on the front steps. Our friend sat with him. They had been friends for as long as he could remember.

"Let me illustrate," old Abe continued. "When I go out into the field to plant corn and my wife, Mandy, goes along with me, I tell her to drop two or three kernels of corn to the hill. No more. No less. And she minds me. 'Cause that's my territory.

"Now after I've finished the day's work and walk into the kitchen with my muddy shoes and Mandy says, 'Now Abe, you get your dirty feet off my kitchen floor!' I mind her — 'cause that's *her* territory!"

Mr. and Mrs. Crosby Adams were highly respected members of our little community.

Actually it was Mr. and *Dr.* Crosby Adams.

She was a nationally acclaimed musician, on one occasion featured in a special event at Soldier Field in Chicago.

Nearing ninety, neither of them drove a car. But we would occasionally see them tottering around Montreat, hand in hand.

When Mrs. Adams was asked to play for the church services, Mr. Adams would gallantly assist her up the stone steps to the platform in Gaither Chapel. And when she was through, he would unsteadily make his way up, take her by the hand, and the whole congregation would hold its breath till both were safely in their pew.

In his eighties, Mr. Adams decided to memorize to keep his mind nimble.

Whenever his wife was asked to play, she would in turn ask him to give a reading, which he did beautifully in his deep, expressively resonant voice, a true professional. She was determined not to upstage him. And he was determined to protect her. So, at his insistence, he washed the dishes for fear the dishwater might cause her fingers to develop arthritis.

I stopped by to take them shopping one day. While Mrs. Adams was getting ready, her husband asked me, "Would you like to know the secret of our happy marriage?" Of course I would.

He led me into their study, where there stood two cluttered rolltop desks; I was surveying these with genuine interest when he explained, "I never disturb her desk. And she never disturbs mine."

"It is impossible to love," it has been said, "someone at whom you cannot laugh."

Whether it is a masculine characteristic or just Bill, I don't know. But he cannot find things he is looking for. Often as not, they are right under his nose.

After we were married, we lived for three years with my parents in Montreat, North Carolina. We had the upstairs back bedroom. One morning, Bill called down sounding thoroughly frustrated. "Ruth, I can't find my trousers." I told him I'd be up shortly, as I was in the middle of helping Mother fix breakfast. When I finally climbed the steps, he was no longer merely frustrated, he was exasperated.

"It's a mighty funny thing!" he exclaimed. "We live in one room. And last night I hung them on the foot of the bed."

I searched the room quickly, then glanced at him. Then I looked again, the light breaking. "Would you happen to be wearing them?" I inquired. Bill looked down at himself. The slow look of disbelief turned quickly into a grin.

This has continued to greater or lesser degrees down through the years.

Last year while we were on vacation, Bill started for his daily walk up the beach. He pulled on his beach shoes over his socks, then couldn't find his watch. We searched everywhere. Finally he borrowed one from our friend Morrie Friedman, and headed off.

An hour later he was back, returned Morrie's watch, and proceeded to remove shoes and socks for a swim.

Out fell his watch.

Pity the married couple who expect too much from one another.

Love stories that end, "And so they were married and lived happily ever after," can be misleading.

I read my old premarriage love poems with a bit of amusement. I wrote them so earnestly — meaning every word — and lived to find them really unfair.

It is a foolish woman who expects her husband to be to her that which only Jesus Christ Himself can be: always ready to forgive, totally understanding, unendingly patient, invariably tender and loving, unfailing in every area, anticipating every need, and making more than adequate provision. Such expectations put a man under an impossible strain.

Since the Christian's Point of Reference is the Bible, it's a happy couple who look there for guidance.

We women learn from the Bible tht God created us to be a "help meet" for our husbands (Genesis 2:18). That is, a help suited to their needs. Since every man is different, needs will vary. So it is up to the wife to study her own husband to discover how she can best meet those needs.

And she is to adapt herself to him. Now, this takes skill and imagination. It keeps a woman feminine.

In fact, some of the most beautiful women I know, as far as character goes, have developed from adapting to difficult men.

But Christian husbands have a tremendous responsibility. They are to love their wives *as Christ loved the Church* and gave Himself for it.

Ellen de Kroon Stamps commented about husbands playing a significant role in the family:

> "Our home these days is more like a hotel .. our table for four is usually too small—but that's what happens when we give little things like a house back to the Master. Bob often talks about a sense in his life that God has called him to be a priest over our household—an awesome but precious responsibility. I've been very thankful of late that he has interpreted his priesthood to include taking the garbage out, changing diapers, cleaning bathtubs, and being up with the children during the night, in addition to helping to draw us ever closer to our Lord!"

We have often said we would not choose to go back to some of those early days of our marriage. Too often, early love is a mirage built on daydreams. Love deepens with understanding, and varying viewpoints expand and challenge one another. So many things improve with age. A recent advertisement read, "Things of true quality need not fear the years—it only improves them." So it is with marriage.

Those who abandon ship the first time it enters a storm miss the calm beyond. And the rougher the storms weathered together, the deeper and stronger real love grows.

We dined in the home of a well-known entertainer one evening. His television show came on just after dinner.

We all arranged ourselves comfortably around the living room and den to watch. He left to watch in another room by himself.

When the show was over and he returned, it was his sweet little wife who met him first, throwing her arms around him, "You were wonderful, dear. Simply wonderful!" And you could tell she meant every word of it.

Love is not only the "union of two forgivers" but also the "union of two good appreciators."

At home.

While I was counseling during the 1954 crusade in London's Harringay Sports Arena, I sat down one night beside a rather attractive young woman and asked if I could be of help to her. She was staring off into space and I couldn't seem to communicate with her.

On the third try, she took a deep breath and said, "I was just wondering what it would be like to wake up and find yourself married to that man!"

"You've asked the right person," I said. "I've been doing it for the past eleven years."

That was, of course, the end of the counseling session. Though I tried to put her at ease, she left rather hurriedly.

Seriously, if I had all the men in the world to pick from, I would still pick Bill. I would still rather see a little bit of him than a whole lot of any other man.

I admire him for being so clear and undeviating in his determination to communicate the Gospel of Christ to a lost world.

For his deep sense of loyalty to his friends.

For his total honesty.

For—after having to look nice when behind the pulpit or before cameras—his complete indifference to personal appearance when relaxing.

For just being himself.

Strange Apparition

In the summer of 1976, while vacationing in Europe, one day I was sitting on the terrace and saw the strangest-looking apparition coming toward me. It was a tall, lean male in bright-red trunks. Now swimming trunks were just about as conspicuous on a European beach as an evening dress would be. But as if that were not enough, he wore laced-up hush puppies, yellow socks, and a baby-blue Windbreaker, topped by a funny yellow hat that was slightly too small for him but rammed down to his ears. And as if that weren't enough, he had on the largest pair of sunglasses I'd ever seen. I was both amused and fascinated, when all of a sudden it dawned on me: "Oh, no, he's mine!"

It was Bill, decked out in all his glory, and I'd give a mint if I only had a photograph of him. No wonder no one recognized him. Oh, they stared all right, but they couldn't figure out just who he was.

It reminded me of the time in another country when we were waiting for the dining room to open at a hotel and saw a group of tourists in a huddle. They kept looking toward us curiously. Finally, one of them detached herself from the group, came over, and said, "Excuse me, but may I ask you a question?" Permission granted, she asked Bill, "Would you happen to be James Arness?"

"No, Ma'am," Bill replied. Whereupon she thanked him and returned to her group.

It is hard on Bill, being recognized in public places so often, but at the same time there are bonuses. So often people stop by and say how they have been helped through his ministry.

In 1949, Bill was holding a meeting in a large tent at Washington and Hill in downtown Los Angeles. There were only two children at the time, so leaving GiGi with Daddy and Mother, I flew to Los Alamos, New Mexico, where I left Anne, fifteen months old, with my sister and brother-in-law, Rosa and Don Montgomery. Then I continued on to Los Angeles to join Bill.

The meeting was scheduled to last for three weeks, but week by week the committee voted to continue for one more week. So week after week the meeting continued.

One day there was a knock at my door, and I opened it to find Rosa and Don standing outside holding Anne. Anne did not know me. I held out my arms to her and she hid her face against Rosa's neck. We had a crib put in my room, and that night I held in my arms a baby girl who, not remembering that I was her mother, sobbed for her aunt.

It was even worse when she saw her father. He didn't know her, either.

There has been a price to pay. I think God warned me by letting me know this instinctively when after my first date with Bill, I knelt and said, "If You let me share his life, I'll consider it the greatest privilege in the world."

It's a good thing I did not know exactly what lay ahead, for I would never have had the nerve to pray such a prayer.

I know a terrific young mother who laughs gaily when talking about separations.

"Law!" she exclaims. "If he didn't leave from time to time, I'd go raving crazy. We both would!"

So don't feel greedy if you want him home all the time (likely as not, you won't have him *all* the time).

And don't feel guilty if on occasion you're glad to see him go. He's probably secretly glad, too. Not for keeps, you understand—just for a breather. It's what Kahlil Gibran refers to when he says, "Let there be spaces in your togetherness."

Memories can fade, rearrange themselves, or grow out of proportion.

I remember Grandmother Bell looking at my then middle-aged father and remarking fondly, "Bless his dear heart! He never caused me a moment's worry in all his life."

And I have heard Bill's mother say something similar about him.

Now both were godly women (extraordinarily so), and therefore truthful.

That is, truthful as far as their memories permitted.

So, as I reminisce about the children and their growing-up years, I am going back to the old diaries, journals, notes, and letters.

Stories and conversations long forgotten have surfaced from pages unread since they were written down in fondness or frustration years and years ago.

As I prepare dinner for guests, I do not empty the pantry for them. I select what I think they will need and enjoy.

And I have done so here, mindful that fresh products beat canned ones, and that the flavor is best brought out by the truth—whether bitter or sweet, salty, or even peppery.

I climbed the hills
through yesterday:
and I am young
and strong again;
my children climb
these hills with me
and all the time
they shout and play;
their laughter fills
the coves among
the rhododendron and the oak
till we have struggled to
the ridge top
where the chestnuts grew.
Breathless, tired, and content
we let the mountain
breeze blow through
our busy minds
and through our hair,
refresh our bodies, hot and spent,
and drink
from some cool mountain spring,
the view refreshing everything—
Infinity, with hills between,
silent, hazy, wild-serene.
Then...
when I return to now
I pray,
"Thank You, God,
for yesterday."

RBG

People ask me if I did not suffer terribly from loneliness when Bill was away. Occasionally I went to bed with his tweed jacket for company.

But there was little opportunity for loneliness with little Grahams underfoot. And with five little Grahams went an assortment of animal friends and an assortment of people friends as well.

I treasure those years. There were the times of unbelievable bliss when a little snugly wrapped bundle would be laid in my arms, and I would lie there studying each tiny pink finger, each damp eyelash, watching the heartbeat in the top of the little head through the soft fuzz of hair.

And with each one I knew instinctively his or her general character: GiGi would be smarter and wiser than I was; Anne was gentle and loving; Bunny (my namesake who got her nickname because she looked like a rabbit when she was born) brought a special touch of joy. She was a Christmas baby. Every mother should have at least one Christmas baby. It makes one feel very close to Mary. Franklin was the first son, and a strapping one at that. And I knew he would be a handful, but would grow to be someone who could be depended upon.

Five years later, Ned arrived: a sort of happy P.S., and I knew that God had given us a final and very special blessing.

The children taught me much as they were growing up: about themselves, about the world around them, about me, and especially about God.

There were the ridiculous times, the poignant and the frustrating and the happy, fun times, and the civil-war times. There were budding romances that didn't bloom, and the final terrific men and women each would marry.

And so the family jumped from five to ten, and now there are fifteen grandchildren.

But I am getting ahead of myself.

Ruth and Billy celebrating their seventeenth wedding anniversary at the Tchividjians' home in Switzerland. Left to right: Franklin, Anne, Billy, Ruth, Gigi, Bunny in center, Ned getting a head start.

"I Wish You Worked in a Hotel!"

It was the spring of 1966. Grace Kelly was in neighboring Asheville for the filming of *The Swan* at the Biltmore Estate.

GiGi, eyes wide with excitement, announced, "Mother, there is this girl at school and her mother works in the dining room of the Battery Park Hotel. And she gets to meet all sorts of famous people. The other night she even met Grace Kelly. Oh, Mother, I wish you worked in a hotel!"

There were times during those years when I thought I did.

Happy housewife.

Help!

Dear Journal,
Reading again from Exodus 33:12-16. This job of training five little Grahams to be good soldiers of Jesus Christ is too big for me, who am not a good soldier myself. Feeling particularly distracted (or I should say overwhelmed and confused) this morning, I have been looking to the Lord asking, "Where, from here?"

Bill will be leaving soon for the San Francisco meeting. And I almost have a sinking feeling. Not altogether a left-behind and left-out sort of feeling, but swamped, knowing that all the things I have depended on others to do, I shall have to do myself.

And things have not been going smoothly. There is a terrible amount of fighting among the children, ugliness and back talk from GiGi, and peevishness on my part backed by sporadic, uncertain discipline. (Mr. Sawyer said in speaking of his mother the other day, "When she said, 'Whoa,' we knew she meant 'whoa!' ")

I am not walking the Lord's way at all. I am doing what I feel like doing rather than what I ought to do. Three verses hit me hard: "She who is self-indulgent is dead even while she lives" (1 Timothy 5:6 RSV), and "The fruit of the Spirit is . . . self-control" (Galatians 5:22, 23).

Self-indulgence is doing what we want rather than what we ought. I had always thought of self-control applying to temper or to drink. But what about the almonds in the pantry, the ice cream and the chocolate sauce, the candy which I know will add unnecessary pounds and make my face break out? What about controlling my tongue? My tone of voice? Standing up straight? Writing letters? All these and many more need controlling.

And I don't look well to the ways of my household. Children well taught even to brushing teeth and keeping rooms straight. Regular family prayers at supper table. Children's clothes kept mended and neat and organized. Getting ready for Sunday on Saturday. Well, there's no use going into it all. It just boils down to the fact that I am not being a good mother.

So I took it to Him this morning. I want above everything to be the kind of person He wants. If He had His undisputed way in me I would be. Everything would solve itself. The place to begin is here, the time to begin is now. And as I reread Exodus 33:12-16, the phrase that jumped out at me, which I had never noticed before, was: "Shew me now Thy way."

P.S. I could not help but chuckle when I read a quote from Mr. Abba Eban in the *London Times* (June 13, 1980): "...Israelis are not renowned for any spontaneous tendency to agree with one another."

(Neither were little Grahams.)

It had been one of those hectic nights, and I had overslept. Without fixing my hair or pausing for makeup, I hurriedly pulled on my bathrobe, lifted Franklin out of his bed without bothering to change him, and set him in the high chair. I proceeded to set the table hurriedly for breakfast so the children would not be late for school.

That morning, every time GiGi opened her mouth to say something, Bunny interrupted. Finally, in exasperation, GiGi slammed down her fork.

"Mother!" she exclaimed. "Between listening to Bunny and smelling Franklin and looking at you, I'm not hungry!"

GiGi in Glasgow. (Photo by Luverne Gustavson.)

Dear Journal,
*It was around bedtime when I heard Franklin crying. GiGi
had choked him for giving Anne his* TV Guide. *She claimed
he had promised all of his to her.*

*My first reaction ws to go upstairs and thrash her, deprive
her of Monday's TV privileges, and no telling what else. I
was angry. Angry at ugliness after so much beauty and
blessing over the weekend. Angry with her, the oldest, for
being so mean and selfish.*

*So I continued nursing Ned and prayed hard for guidance.
ō"Lord, shew me Thy way." Then I called them all downstairs.*

*These TV Guides, apart from their initial usefulness, have
been nothing but a source of contention. They read them,
study the pictures, collect favorites for husbands, brothers,
etc., etc. So I laid down the law. All were to be burned.*

*It was GiGi, of course, who went dramatic on me. She flatly
refused. Said I was stealing. Wished she was back in
Hampden DuBose School. Christian homes were no fun.
And so on and on.*

*So we got on our knees, and each asked the Lord what He
would have us do with the old guides and piles of treasured
pictures. Anne and Bunny "came up" deciding to burn
them. GiGi, however, still insisted Jesus doesn't take away
all our fun, and that He wouldn't mind their keeping the
better pictures.*

But this is all surface. It's her spiritual development about which I am primarily concerned. How to encourage her Bible study and prayer life. How to help her choose His way. And my ability is definitely limited.

I may be able to make her make up her bed, and keep her from bad movies. But I cannot make her be unselfish, loving, and considerate. I can—up to a point—take care of the outside. But I am wholly dependent upon the Lord to work in her heart to "will and to do" His good pleasure.

If only God will enable me to tend to the possible, depending on Him for the impossible.

Supper was over, the small, round dining-room table cleared, and as we washed the dishes and straightened the kitchen, suddenly Gigi, age six, slugged Anne.

So I sentenced her to sit in her chair for five minutes. Forced inactivity for a child who woke up running and went to sleep running was sheer torture.

Without GiGi, her adored playmate, Anne was lost. In a few minutes she slipped up to me, confiding in her soft voice, "Muffa, I said 'stinky.' Can I sit in the chair, too?" Permission granted, she ran happily over to GiGi.

"It's all right, GiGi," she announced in her gentle way. "I will sit with you."

How's that for empathy?

Punishment

There was the time Gigi and I took the bus from Charlotte back to Black Mountain. It was November 6, 1951. She was six.

We boarded the bus in Charlotte and headed for home. She was unendurable, to put it mildly. Nothing suited her and she made no effort at pretending it did.

Two friendly passengers remarked to me that I surely had my hands full.

"If one more passenger comments on your behavior," I hissed in her ear, "you've had it!"

Instant transformation.

But no sooner had we reached the mountain and settled in the little gray house in the valley when she started scrapping with Anne. I knew there lacked only one more straw to break this camel's back. It wasn't long in coming. She sassed me (an item I considered in the "morals" bracket) and, furthermore, flatly contradicted me. That did it. She got it.

She snapped out of her mood as sweet as pie.

That night as we prayed before supper, I asked God to help us be sweet.

Anne looked up.

"Mother," she said in her own gentle, inimitable way, "you aren't a sweet girl. You spank people."

"She has to, Anne!" GiGi interjected authoritatively. "God told her to. If she doesn't punish us when we are bad, God will punish her."

Dear Journal,

Ruth Peale, at the Layman's Institute of Miami (January 13-16, 1960), stated in her most helpful and refreshing address that "the home should be a place of quiet peacefulness."

And so it should. Ours is an island all right—but at times more like Alcatraz, I think.

Furthermore, the Bible backs up Ruth Peale's statement.

"Better is a dry morsel, and quietness therewith, than a house full of sacrifices ["feasting" RSV] with strife" (Proverbs 17:1), and "He that troubleth his own house shall inherit the wind..." (Proverbs 11:29). Knox translation has it: "He shall feed on air, that misrules his own household...", while Lamsa's Aramaic translation puts it, "...he who fails to make his household tranquil shall bequeath the wind to his children..."

This responsibility falls squarely on the mother's shoulders. Uncomfortably, whenever Proverbs speaks of nagging ("It is better to dwell in a corner of the housetop, than..."), it is the woman to whom Solomon is referring. There is no getting around it. The woman creates the atmosphere in the home.

Unfortunately, I seem to have been infected with a kind of deadly spiritual pacifism, an unwillingness to roll up my sleeves and lick the socks off the devil—or die trying. Here is our home. The thing is almost out of hand—scrapping among the children. It may be natural. It is also sinful.

There is a vital difference between "pacifist" and "peace-maker." Occasionally the peacemaker has to whip the daylights out of the troublemakers in order to have peace. And Jesus never said, "Blessed are the pacifists" but "Blessed are the peacemakers."

Isaiah 41:15 on has helped put a bit of "fight" in me. With God's help, we can "thresh the mountains, and beat them small."

Psalms 18:43: "Thou hast delivered me from the strivings of the people..."

Verse 47: "It is God that...subdueth the people under me."

We can lick this evil. With His help we will. A happy, well-disciplined, well-ordered, loving home is our spiritual right.

One day Anne lunched with friends and me at a local hotel, disgruntled because Bunny couldn't go with us. She was rude, boorish, and disagreeable (all in a sweet sort of way). As we got in the car she said, "Mother, I behaved really dreadfully today, didn't I?"

Her conscience still on the job, she came to me at bedtime. "Mother," she begged, "now please tell me everything I did wrong. I want to know. I want to learn."

How often do I come to God at the close of day in that spirit?

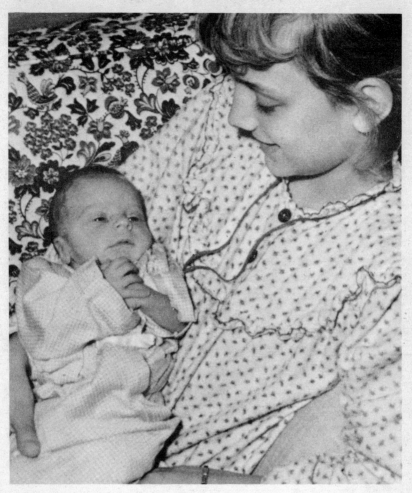

Anne and baby Ned. (Photo by Luverne Gustavson.)

Dear Journal,
Every parent should read at least one good book on dog training. Odd how, in a day when children are notoriously disobedient, dog training and obedience classes are increasing in popularity. Basically the rules are simple.

1. *Keep commands simple and at a minimum. One word to a command and always the same word. Come. Sit. Stay. Heel. Down. No. (I talk my children dizzy.)*
2. *Be consistent.*
3. *Be persistent. Follow through. Never give a command without seeing it is obeyed.*
4. *When the dog responds correctly, praise him. (Not with food. Remember, don't reward children materially for doing well. Your praise should be enough.)*

It is a fine kettle of fish when our dogs are better trained than our children.

The Grahams have always been dog lovers. Here is one of a long succession of family pets. (Photo by Russ Busby.)

I had been extra hard on Anne one day when she was small. The details have evaporated with the years. All, that is, except a small girl's tearful comment as I tucked her in bed, "Mother, you make it so hard to be good!"

Someone has said, "A Christian is one who makes it easy to believe in Jesus."

Perhaps it could also be said, "A good mother is one who makes it easy for a child to be good."

Grandmother with Anne's daughter Morrow.
(Photo by Russ Busby.)

Not Big Enough

Dear Journal,

Problems loom, pressures increase. Because He will be with me, and in the days ahead it will "enjoy my heart" (as Mr. Tchividjian says) to read how He led and overruled and provided, I'll jot some things down.

First, let me note again, I have but one desire for Bill, for our children, and for myself: that we be men and women of God.

Bill walks with God, and God will deal with him. I lie awake nights loathing myself for the person I am, fearful and worried that I cannot bring up this family as I should.

And I can't.

I am a weak, lazy, indifferent character; casual where I should be concerned, concerned where I should be carefree; self-indulgent, hypocritical, begging God to help me when I am hardly willing to lift a finger for myself; quarrelsome where I should be silent, silent where I should be outspoken; vacillating, easily distracted and sidetracked.

> "Thou knowest how soon my mind
> from Heavenly things to earthly
> is drawn aside.
> How oft I fail and fall."

I have found tremendous comfort in this old hymn:

> "Come ye sinners, poor and needy,
> Weak and wounded,
> Sick and sore;

Jesus, waiting, stands to help you,
Full of mercy, love and power...
Let not conscience bid you linger,
Nor of fitness fondly dream;
All the fitness He requireth
Is to feel your need of Him..."
JOSEPH HART

"What would I do," wrote Chalmers, "if God did not justify the ungodly?"

And "What would I do," said Thomas Boston of Scotland, "but for the imputed righteousness?"

There it is. All that I am not, He is; all that I am and should not be, He forgives and covers. But this remains: I am not big enough for the job ahead of me. Not big enough, or strong enough, or wise enough, or loving enough, or selfless enough, or anything enough.

I am thinking in ink—writing to myself, really. For some reason, it helps.

Bill was home more than most people realize, but not as much as we would have liked.

I vividly recall our small, blond-haired girl sitting in the grass, her translucent blue eyes fixed on a plane overhead and far away. In a wistful little voice she was calling, "Bye, Daddy! Bye, Daddy!"

A plane implied that Daddy was on it, going somewhere. How much we missed him, only each one knows.

Bunny was born good. I should write one chapter called "Don't Take Advantage of the Good Child." But perhaps sometimes mothers need to. Perhaps that's why God sends a particularly good one here and there along the line.

Bunny played in her crib by the hour as a baby, never asking for anything. She was the sort of child who kept her room neat without being told, obeyed promptly, and had a marvelous disposition coupled with a ridiculous sense of humor.

Mr. Rickman, who took care of us for many years, cutting the lawn, scraping the snow off the roads in the winter, driving the kids to school in the Jeep, and even helping with the heavy housework, taught each of the children to drive at an early age.

At that time, one of the association's secretaries lived with us. A friend was visiting her. I had to go down to Jackson, Mississippi, to speak at Bel Haven College graduation. On the way back I called home, only to learn that GiGi had driven the whole crowd over the mountain in the Jeep, demolishing it and injuring several passengers—none seriously. Needless to say, the rest of the flight home seemed endless.

I arrived to find Franklin with several stitches in his head, the guest with a badly bruised thigh, the Jeep pretty well totaled, Bunny complaining that her arm hurt, and GiGi near tears at the mention of the mishap.

GiGi had permission to drive from the gate to the house, but I did not know that she was going to extend this from the house, up around the mountain to the distant Reid field, and back. It was on the way back that she hit a spongy spot in the road where water from a little spring crossed. The road gave way and down the Jeep went, turning over several times. We were only grateful that it was not more serious.

Bunny continued to complain about her arm, but since it was neither discolored nor swollen we told her to forget it. But the complaining continued for several weeks. Finally, to settle the matter, I took her to an orthopedic surgeon. An X-ray showed a fractured arm. From then on, whenever Bunny complained, we listened.

As I tucked Bunny in bed one night, she caught my hand and hugged it to her soft little face.

"Mother, you know why I like your hands?" she asked.

"Why?"

"They are so soft and bony, and the skin is so loose on them. Not too loose," she hastened to add, "just right!"

Bunny and friend. (Photo by Luverne Gustavson.)

On hearing indignant wails from the kitchen, I looked in to see what was happening. Bunny, age three, was holding her hand to her cheek and eyeing Anne reproachfully.

"What on earth's the matter?" I demanded.

"Mommy," replied five-year-old Anne patiently, "I'm teaching Bunny about the Bible. I'm slapping her on one cheek and teaching her to turn the other one so I can slap it, too."

Bunny's daugher Noelle and her grandmother.
(Photo by Russ Busby.)

"One, Two, Free"

Franklin, at three, managed to get into everybody's hair. I never knew one small boy could be so omnipresent. He was lovable and stubborn, reserved, surprisingly tender at times, and an incorrigible tease. I have seen all three sisters in tears and Franklin still laughing gleefully.

He went through a spitting stage. I don't know where he picked up that one.

Johnny and Tommy Frist were teenagers then, summering in Montreat. They enjoyed Franklin, and when the rest of us would be ready to send him to the pound, they would still be laughing good-naturedly.

One day, Johnny was up here bantering with Franklin, who had gone through his whole repertoire—spitting and all. Johnny had warned, "You spit one more time and you'll be sorry!"

Franklin spit. So Johnny picked him up and, still chuckling, stuffed him in the woodbin built into the stone wall by the kitchen fireplace, and latched the door.

All was quiet. We looked at one another. Johnny, still grinning, pushed his blond hair back off his forehead and waited.

Soon a small voice said, "Okay. I'll count ten for you t' let me out'n here."

Quiet.

"One. Two. Free—"

Quiet again.

"One. Two. Free—"

Again, silence.

Finally, Johnny broke the silence. "What's the matter in there, Franklin? Why'd you stop?"

"Can't count any higher," he replied, in a somewhat subdued voice.

Music played quietly as the offering plate reached our row. Out of the corner of my eye, I saw Franklin dip his hand into the offering.

Quick as a flash, I grabbed the five-year-old fist.

Looking up, an aggrieved exression on his little-boy face, he exclaimed loud enough for all about to hear, "I was only hiding my penny under his dollar."

Aware of the suppressed smiles around us, I could only think of how often I had been guilty of the same thing: trying to hide my penny under someone else's dollar.

Franklin in Switzerland. (Photo by Luverne Gustavson.)

Ned arrived after we moved up on the mountain.

There is a picture of us in the big old press bed in our room, with Bill and the four older ones watching him with pride and appreciation.

I can still see Franklin, five years old by then, never one to dress up much if he could help it. He clomped as quietly as his cowboy boots let him, guns and holsters slung low around the hips that were barely there, a big glass of milk clutched in both grimy hands, sloshing precariously.

"So you'll have plenty of milk," he explained. —

I refrained from explaining that a cow does not drink milk to make milk. It was the thought that counted.

Nearly three years later, looking out of the upstairs corner window, I saw a picture that impressed itself indelibly on my memory. Franklin was now nearly eight, and Ned, around three.

Abandoning the curvy driveway, they were taking a short-cut straight up the side of the mountain. The steepness was too much for little Ned, who slipped and started to fall. As always, quick on the draw, Franklin caught him, then kneeling down, helped Ned scramble up on his back. Grasping him firmly under the knees, Franklin struggled up the mountain with his added load.

In the intervening years when, because of the difference in age and temperaments, they were not so close, that picture kept coming to mind and I knew that, eventually, that was the way it would be. Not necessarily the older supporting the younger, but each one helping the other.

Dear Journal,
Little Franklin has never, to my knowledge, put his trust
in Christ. Nor do I believe he has rejected Him. And he will
not be pushed, nor do I intend to. But my heart would rest
easier if I knew there was a concern—a conviction of sin. In
fact, I wonder if he is really aware of it, even.

I had a dream about a year ago. Franklin was a young
man— gay, attractive, brushing aside all concern for his
spiritual welfare. Unreachable. I awoke with a dread and a
sickness, only to find it was a dream. He was still a little
boy at home with us.

There is still time.

> *"Love which outlives*
> *All sin and wrong, Compassion which forgives*
> *To the uttermost, and justice whose clear eyes*
> *Through lapse and failure look to the intent*
> *And judge our frailty by the things we meant."*
> **J. G. WHITTIER**

Franklin was polishing his shoes on the hearth. Beatrice Long, who helped us for over thirty years, overheard him ask Ned, "Ned, do you love me?"

Ned answered thoughtfully.

"Yes, Nock. My love you."

"Well," came the heartless reply, "I don't love you."

Ned leaned back against the stone hearth, and thought a minute. "Well, I love you."

"Well, I don't love you."

"The Bible says—"

Franklin cut him off.

"The Bible doesn't say I have to love you, does it?"

"Well . . . the Bible says some nice things."

Franklin had Ned trained to stand outside his door rather than entering. One night as I was tucking Franklin in, a small, pajamaed figure appeared at the door.

"Nock, can I come in and kiss you good-night?" Permission granted, he did, and trotted off to bed.

"You know," Franklin confided to me, "he's a pretty good little boy."

Ned at a friend's home in Switzerland. (Photo by Luverne
Gustavson.)

How often our children reflect our attitudes.

Ned was three and a half years old.

"My playing school," he announced.

"Is it fun?" I asked unnecessarily, as he was obviously enjoying himself.

"No," he replied with a sigh, "it's *hard* work!"

Tucking Ned in bed one night, I leaned down to kiss him good-night.

Looking closely at my face, a delighted smile spread over his.

'It looks just like sunshine," he said.

"What looks like sunshine?" I asked.

And his fingers gently touched the lines going out from the corners of my eyes.

With such an observation, how could anyone mind growing old?

Dear Journal,
Ned, almost five, angelic face (complete with blond hair and large blue eyes), slendering little-boy figure, fast losing his baby chubbiness; our sweet, gentle, loving Ned has developed a quick, violent temper, and just recently a tender, repentant conscience to match.

Recently there was a violent outburst over bedtime. First he refused to go to bed. Then he hit me in the face with a rubber band (he was a crack shot), then he dug me in the stomach with his elbow. So I marched him upstairs, upended and spanked him. Result: He hit me. Another spanking.

Crying copiously, he crawled in bed, pinching my finger as he did.

This I thought best to ignore.

I prayed with him, tucked him in bed, and, my kiss being repulsed, cut out the light and retired quietly. Then his conscience began to work.

"Mom. Come here, please."

Mom came.

"My sorry my hit you."

"Okay. I love you." I kissed him and left.

"Mom. Come here, please."

Mom came again.

"Mom. My just sorry my hit you. My not sorry my pinched your finger."

"Okay. I love you anyway. Good night."

Five minutes later.

"Mom. Come here, please." *(Mom should keep trim as Ned grows up.)*

"My sorry my pinched your finger, too. My love you, Mom."

"My love you, Ned. We're friends, aren't we?"

"Uh-huh."

And conscience clear, sleep came.

There were times in kindergarten when things got rough for Ned.

"There's one boy at school what'n I don't like."

"Why?"

"Him always picks on me."

"How?"

"Every time my knock his blocks down," Ned explained indignantly, "him tells the teacher on me."

"Mom, you know when Martha Luther King was here this summer?" Ned asked.

"Yes."

"Well, some of the children in the clubs, you know? Some of them said to me, 'Martha Luther King is gooder 'n your daddy.' And I said, 'Aw, shut up!' "

"That wasn't very nice," I remonstrated. "They have a right to their own opinons."

"Then," he continued, ignoring my reaction, "you know what I *think* happened?"

"What?"

"I *think* I hit one of them."

"Ned!" I exclaimed sharply. "That really wasn't nice."

Ned's eyes danced gleefully. "And you know what?"

"What?"

"I enjoyed it, too!"

Christmas one year was, we decided, going to be more spiritual and less commercial than usual.

Christmas morning dawned clear and bright. The tree celebrated with lights and ornaments. The mantel over the fireplace was hung from end to end with bulging stockings that sagged onto the hearth beneath, while the gifts under the tree not only overflowed onto the window seat of the broad picture window behind it but spilled halfway across the living-room floor.

Stephan and GiGi and their children had joined us, together with Anne and Danny and theirs. We decided we should have breakfast first so that Beatrice Long, helping, could get on with preparations for Christmas dinner. Sitting down around the breakfast table, we proceeded with sweet rolls, orange juice, coffee, and, for those who liked it, the traditional oyster stew.

The children sat through this patiently. Then Bill decided that we should have devotions before we opened the stockings and gifts. The children accepted this, too, with resignation. Bill assured them that prayers would be brief, but what is brief to a grown-up is not necessarily brief to a child. The devotions seemed to extend unusually long.

But the straw that broke the camel's back came when Anne asked the children to file slowly down the two steps into the living room so that she could get moving pictures of them as they entered the living room.

Stephan Nelson, age five, was standing beside me, his back turned and his arms folded across his chest. Giving a deep sigh of disgust, he exclaimed under his breath, "Bethlehem was never as miserable as this!"

There will be less someday —
much less,
and there will be More;
less to distract
and amuse;
More, to adore;
less to burden
and confuse;
More, to undo
the cluttering of centuries,
that we might view
again, That which star
and angels
pointed to;
we shall be poorer —
and richer;
stripped — and free;
for always there will be a Gift,
always a Tree!

Dear Journal,
*Never let a single day pass without saying an encouraging
word to each child.*

*Particularly wherever you have noticed any—even the
slightest—improvement on some weak point. Some point
at which you have been picking and criticizing.*

*And never fail to pass on any nice thing you have heard said
about anyone, to that child.*

*In David's prayer for Solomon, he said, "... prayer also
shall be made for him continually; and daily shall he be
praised" (Psalms 72:15).*

*"More people fail for lack of encouragement," someone
wrote, "than for any other reason."*

The rumble of thunder was only a distant threat. But the wind in the firs beside the stream, and the oaks and the pines between the bedroom window and the street, announced the storm was on its way.

All my life I have loved storms. But then, I have only experienced them from the shelter of a solidly built house, and as a child, with the warm conviction that with Mother and Daddy near, nothing really bad could happen.

The wind rose menacingly, and there was a sudden crack of thunder directly overhead. Soon I heard the patter of little feet and sensed a small presence in the room. I heard a whispered, "Mother?" That was all.

The covers were thrown back in comforting welcome as one or more small, night-clad forms would slip in (depending on the severity of the storm). There, lovingly encircled, we snuggled safely together under the covers, listening to the storm, unafraid. As nature once more grew quiet, we drifted off to sleep.

It was later, when I knew they were all enduring their own individual storms, that I lay awake wishing I could share them.

At night, it was if I could hear a whispered, "Mother?" Only there was no one there. I sensed the distant thunder, and all I could do was pray.

Like other shepherds
help me keep
watch o'er my flock by night;
mindful of each need,
each hurt, which might
lead one to stray—
each weakness
and each ill—
while others sleep
teach me to pray.
At night wolves and leopards,
hungry and clever, prowl
in search of strays
and wounded; when they howl,
Lord, still
my anxious heart
to calm delight—
for the Great Shepherd
watches with me
over my flock
by night.

RBG

"Look, Mom!" Franklin called excitedly. "Look! The clouds broke to pieces and one got lost!"

I looked out across the valley and, sure enough, the passing storm was dissipating and a little cloud had gotten lost in one of the coves.

Little did we know that the time would come years later when we were the clouds and Franklin got lost.

There were calls from school principals, headmasters, irate teachers, even the police. The last called indignantly one night to say that Franklin had slammed the gate to our property in his face.

I urged the policeman to come up for a talk, assuring him that the gate would be open and I would have a pot of coffee ready. Franklin was, as usual, totally unrepentant and grinning like a possum. Apparently he had passed the local policeman, who had either caught him speeding or thought (from force of habit) he was speeding and took off after him. Whereupon Franklin stepped on the gas and made it to the property in time to slam the electric gate and walk in the house chuckling.

I'm not sure teenagers always appreciate the value of the police.

Years ago during college, when we summered with Grandmother Bell in the Shenandoah Valley of Virginia, my sister Rosa and I taught Daily Vacation Bible School up in the mountains. I was teaching my little group the Beatitudes and one day called on one of them to recite. The only mistake I remembered was, "Blessed are the policemakers," and I'm not sure it was a mistake.

Anyway, the policeman showed up shortly. We sat around the kitchen fire drinking coffee and discussing various subjects, finally getting around to the situation. To this day, I don't know whether Franklin was speeding or not. I'm not even convinced the policeman was convinced. But we did apologize for the gate slammed in his face, which Franklin considered fun, I considered rude, and the policeman considered infuriating. And that particular episode came to a friendly conclusion.

But there were other episodes, other complaints, other phone calls.

A columnist quoted the following: "Columnist Charles McHarry writes that the handsome lad nightclubbing in New York with Gayle Horne, Lena's daughter, was Billy Graham, Jr., son of the evangelist."

I saved this as a reminder to myself and as a bit of concrete evidence to lay before the Lord. We got a laugh out of it. It was all so absurd. Franklin was only nine years old. And the columnist himself printed a retraction of it.

The sobering fact is that it shows none of our children can ever live really privately—succeed privately or sin privately.

If God will graciously satisfy each child *early* with His mercy, that they may rejoice and be glad *in Him* all their days (Psalms 90:14), this will be enough.

"There is no situation so chaotic that God cannot, from that situation, create something that is surpassingly good. He did it at the creation. He did it at the cross. He is doing it today."

BISHOP MOULE

It was early in the morning in another country. Exhausted as I was, I awoke around three o'clock. The name of someone I loved dearly flashed into my mind. It was like an electric shock. Instantly I was wide awake. I knew there would be no more sleep for me the rest of the night. So I lay there and prayed for the one who was trying hard to run away from God. When it is dark and the imagination runs wild, there are fears that only a mother can understand.

Suddenly the Lord said to me, *Quit studying the problems and start studying the promises.* Now God has never spoken to me audibly, but there is no mistaking when He speaks.

So I turned on the light, got out my Bible, and the first verse that came to me was Philippians 4:6, "Be careful for nothing; but in every thing by prayer and supplication *with thanksgiving* let your requests be made known unto God." And verse 7, "And the peace of God, which passeth all understanding, shall keep your hearts and minds through Christ Jesus." Or, as the Amplified Version has it, "Do not fret or have any anxiety about anything, but in every circumstance and in everything by prayer and petition [definite requests] *with thanksgiving* continue to make your wants known to God . . ." (my italics).

Suddenly I realized the missing ingredient in my prayers had been "with thanksgiving." So I put down my Bible and spent time worshiping Him for who He is and what He is. This covers more territory than any one mortal can comprehend. Even contemplating what little we do know dissolves doubts, reinforces faith, and restores joy. I began to thank God for giving me this one I loved so dearly in the first place. I even thanked Him for the difficult spots which taught me so much.

And you know what happened? It was as if suddenly someone turned on the lights in my mind and heart, and the little fears and worries which, like mice and cockroaches, had been nibbling away in the darkness, suddenly scuttled for cover.

That was when I learned that worship and worry cannot live in the same heart. They are mutually exclusive.

Dear Journal,
I cannot sleep. For a while I sat here in bed with the lights off, and thought and prayed. I have a headache. It would be so easy to take a sleeping pill, but He knows I need sleep— and how much. And sometimes there are more important things. Like seeing the world outside flooded with moon- light and watching the last log in my fireplace flicker and die, the shadows of the ceiling beams leaping, as it were, in the firelight. And knowing He is here.

I've taken time out to remember all this because of one special thing He said. He has told it to me before, many times, in one way or another.

It's about Franklin.

Every time I pray, especially for wisdom to discipline him, God says, Love him more.

I get snowed with my responsibility at times, and when I do, I fret. And as always it "tends only to evil" (Psalms 37:8 RSV). I get cross and take it out on the kids. Not deliber- ately. But I am worried about not being a better mother and then I nag or scold when I should just instruct or correct.

Well, every time I start talking to the Lord about Franklin, God keeps saying, Love him. *Which seems (or could seem) odd—because I love every bone of him. But God means "show it." Let him in on the fact. Enjoy him. You think he's the greatest—let him know you think so.*

My head is trying to wise up my heart.

The heart worries, fears the worst, imagines all sorts of things, wants to guide, counsel, control, choose.

The head says, "Lay off. Trust God. Love Franklin. Be sympathetic, understanding, patient, confident. Let him know you have confidence in him. Turn loose. And pray."

> "Do I find love so full in my nature, God's
>   ultimate gift,
> That I doubt his own love can compete with it?
>   Here, the parts shift?
> Here, the creature surpass the Creator—the
>   end, what Began?
> Would I fain in my impotent yearning do all for
>   this man,
> And dare doubt he alone shall not help him,
>   who yet alone can?"

From Saul
ROBERT BROWNING

I fell out of a tree.

Most people, on hearing that, hesitate to ask, "What on earth were you doing up a tree?"

I was, as a matter of fact, building a pipe slide for the grandchildren then living in Mequon, Wisconsin.

Now a properly built pipe slide can be great fun, but I'm not going to tell you how to build one, for fear you might.

The Mequon hardware was somewhat limited in materials. However, we got the slide assembled. But before letting the grandchildren try it, I made a test run.

I woke up a week later in the hospital with my left heel shattered, one rib broken, a crushed vertebra in my neck, and a concussion.

When I first hit the ground and lay still, the grandchildren and GiGi, our daughter, thought I was playacting. After they had coaxed, "Come on, you've carried this far enough," their Doberman came and licked me across the face. When there was no response from me, they realized I was out for real, and flew to the house to get Stephan, GiGi's husband. He carried me indoors and called the only doctor nearby, a friend who also happened to be a psychiatrist.

I was in shock by then, so their friend called an ambulance, checked me into a hospital, then turned me over to the orthopedic surgeons.

I could not have been in better hands, and eventually recovered.

Months later, when Bill was holding crusades in Texas, this psychiatrist friend visited the meetings, sitting on the platform one evening.

On that occasion, on nationwide television, my husband announced matter-of-factly, "My wife fell out of a tree and tonight her psychiatrist is here on the platform."

Can you believe that? And on nationwide television.

Calvin, as he is affectionately known to everyone around here, has been pastor of the Montreat Presbyterian Church for nearly twenty years. Apart from gardening, he enjoys hunting for recreation. I question whether he ever catches anything, for if there is anything Calvin likes to do better than garden or hunt, it is to talk.

Calvin used to take Franklin out once a week for target practice. When he heard about the powerful new pistol someone had given Bill, he decided he'd better come up and show Franklin exactly how to handle it and how not to handle it, and they disappeared around the Jeep trail that led to the old Reid field in the next cove.

Supper was ready when the door opened and Franklin slipped in. I heard Calvin's car roar down the mountain. Franklin sat down at the table quietly.

"Aren't you hungry?" I asked, noticing he didn't touch his food.

"No, Ma'am," he said. This was unlike him.

Finally I asked, "Is everything all right?"

"Yes, Ma'am," he replied with uncharacteristic brevity.

Later I tried once more.

"Did you and Calvin have some sort of disagreement?"

"No, Ma'am."

Supper over and the dishes washed up, I headed toward my

bedroom, saying as I went, "If there's anything you'd like to talk over with me, I'll be in my room."

It wasn't long before the phone rang.

Calvin's deep Southern drawl on the other end said laconically, "Well, I guess Franklin told you what happened."

"I can't get the boy to say one single word," I replied, "except 'Yes, Ma'am' and 'No, Ma'am.'"

"Well," the Texas drawl continued, "I shot myself."

"You *what?*"

Then Calvin went on to describe how he had had the gun in his holster and had just finished saying, "Franklin, never do this." Whipping the gun out of the holster, he accidentally touched the trigger. There was a loud explosion and Calvin doubled over, clutching his leg.

To Franklin's persistent demand, "What's the matter? What's the matter?" Calvin growled, "I shot myself—and if you say one word about it, I'll never take you shooting again."

It isn't often you find a pastor so concerned with members of his congregation that he will give them such a valuable object lesson. And all the sympathy poor Calvin got when he limped out onto the platform for the Sunday morning service was a wave of laughter from his congregation.

Not everyone around Franklin was an inspiration.

At one conference, he watched a difficult Christian leader repeatedly rebuke, correct, and embarrass an older Christian who happened to be working under him.

"No person is absolutely unnecessary," someone has said. "One can always serve as a horrible example."

Day after day, Franklin quietly watched and listened, unable to intervene.

Not once did the older man show anything but Christian graciousness and humility. Never once did he get angry and complain. Not once did he strike back. He was a perfect illustration of Rotherham's translation of Proverbs 24:25, "To reprovers one should be pleasant."

Neither the "horrible example" nor the gentle saint was aware he was being observed. Neither knew the scales in one young heart were being tilted inevitably toward the Saviour because of an older man's close resemblance to Him when under attack.

There are times to yell.

Our house was in the process of being built. The living room, the largest room in the house, was set up as a sort of carpenter's shop. In the center sat a large table saw with a revolving blade.

I was relying heavily on Chamberlain's *New England Interiors* and any of his other books I could find, for ideas on finishing the inside of the house.

One day, book in hand, I went in search of Mr. Gregg Sawyer and Zeb, his brother. They both were master craftsmen.

I found them in the living room and held out the book for them to see a certain picture.

Suddenly both men yelled at me.

I froze, incredulous. Perfect gentlemen, they had always treated me with courtesy. Now this—

Then I saw. I had come upon them unexpectedly, and Mr. Zeb had not flipped the switch to shut off the motor to the revolving blade. My hand, holding the book, was only inches away from the blade, of which I was unaware, and I had begun to lower the book.

It was their yelling that saved my hand, and I shall be forever grateful!

I know a mother whose child was about to make a tragic mistake. She yelled so vehemently that the child moved away, and it was months before he would communicate with his mother. Then God intervened, the crisis passed, and they are now in that happily-ever-after stage. This mother confided to me how guilty she felt for having yelled.

"Sometimes," I replied, "a mother has to." I pointed out that while she might have made her son angry, it kept him from making a tragic mistake, for which he will be eternally grateful.

Yelling cannot replace praying, but each has its place.

Looking back over the years, the children may be able to remember the times when Bill and I had to yell—for their sakes. I'm only hoping that they will look back, as I do to the Sawyer brothers, with gratitude.

We were just beginning family prayers one morning, gathered around the fireplace in the kitchen, when Mr. Sawyer, our contractor, came in. (We had moved into this house before it was quite finished.)

Now Mr. Sawyer was an old family friend. He had remodeled Mother and Daddy's home for them; he had remodeled our first little house in the valley; he had remodeled the little cabin on the mountain before we built this house. He had undertaken to do this one, which was somewhat more complicated, being built largely from scratch out of old log cabins and material salvaged from old houses.

But I am getting sidetracked. This is not about salvaging old materials but salvaging a boy.

Mr. Sawyer, clad in his crumpled khaki pants and plaid shirt, poked his unshaven face in the kitchen door. We explained that we were just beginning family prayers, and asked him to join us. That day I had passed around small cards, on each of which was printed a Scripture verse. We would go around the room, each child and adult taking a turn reading the verse on his or her card.

Now Mr. Sawyer had the interesting habit of cleaning his glasses between his thumb and forefinger. At times, noticing the cloudy condition of the glasses, I marveled that he was able to see through them. His verse that morning was, "Whom the Lord loveth He chasteneth..." (*see* Hebrews 12:6).

But the way Mr. Sawyer read it, it came out, "Whom the Lord loveth, He chaseth."

It was just what I needed.

For Franklin, the "Hound of Heaven" was closing in.

How long ago was that? Yesterday? Twenty-five years ago?

Franklin just called to check on me. When Bill is away, he calls from time to time to make sure I am all right. I appreciate it.

Franklin has a terrific little wife now, and his own three sons — "as good as they can be, and as bad as they can get away with," just like he was. He deserves each one. And may they give him as much fun (and frustration) as he gave me — and as much joy when they are grown.

God,
look who my Daddy is!
He is the one
who wore his guardian angel out
(he thought it fun).
First, it was bikes:
he tore around those hills
like something wild,
breaking his bones
in one of many spills;
next, it was cars:
how fast he drove (though well)
only patrolmen
and his guardian angel knew;
the first complained,
the second never tells.
Then it was planes:
that was the closest we
ever got—till now.
I never knew him well
except that he
kept that angelic guardian
on his toes.

Not long ago
You touched him,
and he turned,
Oh, Lord, what grace!
(And how quizzical the look
upon his angel's face:
a sort of skidding-to-a-stop
to change his pace.)

And now, he just had me:
which only shows
who needs a little angel of his own
to keep *him* on *his* toes.
Oh, humorous vengeance!
Recompense—with fun!
I'll keep *him* busy, Lord.
Well done! Well done!   RBG

Left to right: William Franklin Graham III, IV, II.
(Photo by Russ Busby.)

Little Black Lamb

I was reading Psalms 139:7-12, putting a certain loved name in appropriately. Suddenly I realized this was another side of Luke 15—the parable of the lost sheep.

With such a Shepherd, that lost sheep hadn't a chance.

When Franklin was born, Luverne Gustavson, Bill's secretary at that time, gave him a little stuffed black lamb containing a music box which, when wound, played "Jesus Loves Me." It is on the bookshelf in my bedroom now beside a picture of Franklin in Israel holding a little black lamb.

Prophetic? Almost.

A comfort? Frequently.

> Fleeing from You
> nothing he sees
> of Your going before him
> as he flees.
>
> Choosing his own paths
> how could he know
> Your hand directs where
> he shall go?
>
> Thinking himself free
> —free at last—
> unaware Your right hand
> holds him fast.

Waiting for darkness
to hide in night,
not knowing, with You
dark is as light.

Poor prodigal!
seeking a "where" from "whence"...
how does one escape
Omnipotence?

RBG

Much has been written and said about the Prodigal Son.

What about the parents?

I have seen them at times — bravely facing other parents who, like them, had done everything right; and whose children had chosen to follow Christ, while theirs had rejected the Truth and gone.

How, I wondered, did Monica, the mother of Augustine, feel among her friends during those years when her brilliant young son, a leader of the heretical "Manichees," lived in open defiance of God and the Church? (*See Augustine*, by Louis Bertrand.)

How did Jim Vaus's parents feel? His father was an ordained Baptist minister, yet his son was repeatedly caught cheating or stealing, all the while charading as a Christian. After a stint in the navy, he received a dishonorable discharge and eventually wound up seriously involved with the underworld network of crime.

> They felt good eyes upon them
> and shrank within — undone;
> good parents had good children
> and they — a wandering one.
>
> The good folk never meant
> to act smug or condemn,
> but having prodigals
> just "wasn't done" with them.
>
> Remind them gently, Lord,
> how You
> have trouble with Your children,
> too.
>
> RBG

After the rare and heady experience of spending a night at the White House, Bill and I had to go to New York City.

As we walked into our room, the maid said, "This room ain't ready yet. You get out and I'll tell you when it's done."

We got!

She was watching her favorite soap opera. When it was finished, so was she.

Back to earth in a hurry!

God has delightful ways of keeping us on an even keel.

There were three of us standing together in one corner of the lovely Palm Beach home of some dear friends who had given a reception for Bill and me: the young wife of a local politician, a prominent businessman, Colonel Paul, and myself.

The young wife was enthusiastically telling us how God always helped her whenever she asked Him, how many prayers He answered for her, and how He always got her out of a jam.

Colonel Paul listened attentively, his eyes twinkling. When there was an adequate pause in the conversation, he took advantage of it and said simply, eyes still twinkling, "I often think there is only one of You" [looking up expressively] "and so many of us" [extending his arms to include the world with its millions of mortals]. "Please—what can I do to help You today?"

Since then, I have started many a day with that simple prayer, "Lord, what can I do to help You today?"

"Where do you think you're going?" was printed at the bottom of my hotel receipt in a neat, boxed-in area.

Good question. Fortunately, I knew. Or thought I knew.

Leaving the Mayo Clinic, friends who had gone through at the same time insisted on having their pilot fly me to Milwaukee in their plane.

"No way," I replied. "It's not that far. I'll go commercial."

"It's settled. John will fly you and pick us up on the way back." And I knew it was useless to argue.

We were all having breakfast together in the coffee shop and John, undoubtedly one of the world's best pilots and ready to fly anywhere at the drop of a hat, agreed readily.

So we flew. Before I had time to finish my illustrated thank-you note to pin on the window curtain, we landed.

I deplaned. No Stephan and GiGi, who were supposed to meet me.

"I'd better hang around a bit till they show up," John said uneasily.

"Oh, they'll show up. They're probably just late."

Finally, at my insistence, John boarded the plane and taxied down the runway.

Half and hour later, I went to the desk and asked to have Stephan and GiGi paged at the large airport across the airfield.

No answer.

So I called their house.

"What city is that in?" the operator asked.

"Mequon."

"Mequon? I have no Mequon listed."

Dumb operator, I thought.

"It's a suburb of Milwaukee," I explained patiently.

"Oh," the voice said, "that will be long distance."

Long distance is surely getting short, I thought.

When Cathy, their live-in help answered, she said they had left early and were at the airport waiting.

"Commercial or private?" I asked.

"Private."

"Well, I'm here, and they're not. I'll just wait."

An hour later—

Slowly, an uneasy feeling began to stir around inside me.

Going back to the desk, I looked at the girl, shook my head, and asked, "Please—could you tell me what city I'm in?"

"Minneapolis," she replied.

Come to think of it, nothing was said about where I was going, except to see GiGi. John knew Bill's headquarters was in Minneapolis. And Milwaukee and Minneapolis both begin with *M*. No one ever figured out exactly what happened.

But he's still one of the world's best pilots!

Anyway, it's important not only to know where you are, but that hotel was pretty smart to ask, "Where do you think you're going?"

Spiritually, I mean.

Especially when our final Destination is *final.*

Colleen Evans, in her challenging book *Start Loving*, quotes a friend who had written her:

> "Our failures. That's the hardest area, especially when they have affected the lives of our loved ones. As our two children step out into the adult world it is a joy to see many beautiful things in their lives. But it hurts to see areas of need and struggle that stem in part from ways we have failed them.
>
> "A friend reminded me recently that even these areas are part of the 'all things' which God will use to make a man and a woman who will accomplish His unique purposes.
>
> "So when thoughts of my failures push their way into my consciousness, I let His total forgiveness dissolve my regrets, and go on to praise Him who accepts us just as we are and lovingly works to make us more than we are."

And from the same book, "He doesn't expect us—or our children—to be finished products now."

Some fishermen in the highlands of Scotland came into a little Scottish inn late one afternoon for a cup of tea. As one was describing "the one that got away" to his friends, he flung out his hands in the typical fisherman's gesture. He did so just as the waitress was setting down his cup of tea. The resulting collision left a huge tea stain spreading on the whitewashed wall. The fisherman apologized profusely.

Another gentleman seated nearby said, "Never mind."

Rising, he took a crayon from his pocket and began to sketch around the ugly brown stain. Slowly there emerged the head of a magnificent royal stag with antlers spread. He was Landseer, England's foremost painter of animals.

Now if an artist can do that with an ugly brown stain, what can God do with my sins and mistakes if I but give them to Him?

Dryness

Bill was away in Rio de Janeiro addressing the Baptist World Alliance that summer.

My job was to pack five little Grahams and myself for a summer to be spent in Switzerland. (I offered to go and address the Baptists while he packed and prepared the five little Grahams for Switzerland, but the idea was not received with enthusiasm.)

Only a mother who has tried to pack for herself plus five children for several months in a foreign country will know the difficulty of the job.

Finally, preparations were finished and we departed for Switzerland. After a long and tiring day, the plane landed in Geneva. We were met by the Tchividjians, our hosts for the summer.

I was too tired that night to notice much. I just felt the warmth of their welcome and the coolness of the linen sheets after everyone had departed and the children had been safely tucked in bed.

The next morning when I woke and pulled up the rolling blinds, I found myself looking out over Lake Geneva and the snowcapped mountains beyond rising to the majestic Dents du Midi. Everything was utterly charming and peaceful.

That is, until the children woke up. Keeping house in Europe, I found, is considerably different from keeping house in America. Grocery shopping needed to be done every day. Not only that, instead of supermarkets there were small shops for each particular item: the butcher shop, cheese shop, grocery, fruit stand, and so forth. Our bread was delivered daily to us freshly baked, unwrapped, sticking out of the basket on the back of the bread boy's bicycle. Long, skinny French loaves, crusty on the outside, light and scarce on the inside.

So I found a good part of my time taken up simply in keeping the family fed and the house run. The result? Spiritual drought.

For me, spiritual dryness usually follows an extremely busy period. Air must be still for dew to fall, and I was anything but still.

One day, Bob and Myrl Glockner, who were spending the summer in a nearby hotel, came by, collected our five children and GiGi's high school roommate, Dorothy Mayell, who was our houseguest, and took them off for the day.

I grabbed my Bible, found an empty chaise on the portico leading from the dining room to the front yard, and there, in the sun, I read Job all day.

I felt like the prophet, fed by angels in the desert when he had reached the end of himself—fed and refreshed. And, we are told, he went in the strength of that food forty days and nights.

When the car pulled up the drive and through the iron gates late that afternoon, all the occupants piled out, tired but happy, full of the day's experiences. Supper was waiting, and their mother was refreshed and eager to have them back.

Drifting ... slipping ... slow I went;
no leap in sudden haste,
but quietly I eased away
into this silent waste.

How long it's been, I do not know;
a minute from Him seems
like long midnights of emptiness,
and silent screams.

I heard the distant promises
with wistfulness; and groped to see
a glimmer of Him in the dark:
Could He see me?

There was no pounding on the Gates,
—no cry at Heaven's door...
I had no strength; my tears left
a puddle on the floor.

Then from my crumpled nothingness,
my dungeon of despair,
a quiet opening of the door
—a breath of Living air.

He let me sleep, as if I'd died,
yet when the morning broke
the Risen Son discovered me,
and I awoke.

New, I awoke; His warming love,
updrawing, transformed everything.
Tell me—is this how an acorn feels
in Spring?

RBG

Although their father, whom our children loved and admired enormously, was away from home so much, their grandfather lived just across the road during the early part of their lives, and just down the mountain until his death in 1973. He was a tremendous father figure.

He loved each grandchild and had a deep concern for all of them. During that period in Franklin's life when he had not only lost interest in spiritual things but school as well, Daddy was prayerful.

After he died, I retrieved a leather-bound *Cruden's Concordance* which Bill and I had given him some years before. In this we found one of his prayer lists. Most of it was illegible. (Doctors scribble!)

Daddy died August 2, 1973.

Franklin called me August 2, 1978, to tell me he had passed all of his exams and graduated from college. It was some time later, when I was using Daddy's old concordance, that I came across that prayer list again and noticed the only legible item on the list. "Franklin—school." Five years to the day after entering Glory, Daddy's prayer was answered.

Ned had reached the point in life when he wanted a bicycle more than anything.

He had been playing with Joel Barker that fall, and wanted one just like Joel's.

"Today!"

"No," Bill said. "Wait until Christmas."

And that was that.

So Joel lent Ned his new bike for a week. Before the week was over, Ned knew that Joel's bike would be too small for him in a few months.

So he decided he needed a larger, ten-speed model.

The next week he saw one advertised in Sears with:

> three speeds
> stick shift
> spring suspension
> butterfly handles
> triple brakes
> slicks
> —the works!

This was the one he *had* to have (and it was still two months until Christmas)!

Then I understood, as never before, why God does not answer all of our prayers right away.

Today we may be beseeching Him for things which we would not want six months from now.

However, most of our prayers are not "bicycle prayers."

When we pray according to God's will (that the prodigal may return; that the sorrowing may find His comfort; that He will work each situation out for our good and His glory), He hears us. For we know that each of these requests is what He wants.

But at times He has us wait for the answers.

The command "Wait on the Lord" found in Psalms 27:14, reads in the old Prayer Book Version (which is older than our King James Version), "O tarry thou in the Lord's leisure."

And to many of us impatient souls, how "leisurely" He seems at times!

"Faith can read love in God's heart
when His face frowns."
                    JAMES RENWICK
                Scottish Covenanter

 There are times when the question *Why?* is literally wrenched from a person — even an earnest believer.

When I was a child, one of our missionaries committed suicide. Overworked and under unbearable pressure, this dear Christian broke.

And there was the time Uncle Ed and Aunt Gay Currie's little John Randolph, left briefly untended, fell into a tub of scalding water prepared for the week's laundry. Not too long after this, their little daughter, Lucy Calvin, ate poison beans and died.

Uncle Jack Vinson, who wrote to inform the mission family of the tragedy, told of going to comfort Aunt Gay (Uncle Ed was out in the countryside at the time), and of returning, having been comforted by her, instead.

Little did we know in how short a time Uncle Jack would be killed by bandits. And it was Uncle Ed who went out and retrieved his body, not only shot but beheaded as well.

In high school in Korea, one of our fellow students was killed one night by a train. It threw a pall over the entire student body.

So down through life from time to time:

> "The cry of man's anguish goes up to God,
> Lord, take away pain."

And still pain—unexpected, unendurable, and unexplained—continues to strike.

Our older son, Franklin, and his flight instructor were miraculously saved from a plane crash one night (but that's *his* story). The next year, this same instructor was killed in a plane crash.

Nor has the team "family" been exempt: one son accidentally shot by his cousin, a daughter left a vegetable from illicit drugs, the death of an ideal son on the operating table, an unexplainable suicide, broken marriages, runaways...

Is it wrong to ask why? I wondered.

Turning to my concordance, I began to look up Bible references. In Exodus 5:22, Moses asked, "Why?"

And God's only answer was, "Now shalt thou see what I will do" (Exodus 6:1).

Even our Lord asked, "Why?" once—on the cross.

Someone has said that faith never asks why. But surely when pushed beyond endurance, one often involuntarily cries, "Why?"

I believe, like a character in Elie Wiesel's book *Night,* we must "pray for courage to ask the right questions."

You might even get some interesting answers.

But if God chooses to remain silent, faith is content.

I lay my "whys"
before Your Cross
in worship kneeling,
my mind too numb
for thought,
my heart beyond
all feeling:

And worshiping,
realize that I
in knowing You
don't need a "why."

RBG

> Coleridge said he believed the Bible
> to be the word of God because, as he
> put it, "It finds me."

It could be merely a piece of plywood stretched across two sawhorses. But have a special place for Bible study that doesn't have to be shared with sewing or letter writing or the paying of bills. For years, mine was just an old wooden table between an upright chest of drawers and a taller desk. This year I fixed myself a permanent office upstairs, and my Bible study in the bedroom is now a big rolltop desk I have had for years.

But on this desk I have collected a number of good translations of the Bible for reference, a Bible dictionary, a concordance, and several devotional books. I also keep notebooks, a mug full of pens, and one particular Rapidograph pen, with a point like a needle, that writes on India paper without smearing or going through.

When we were in school, we always kept a notebook handy to take notes on the professor's lecture. How much more important it is to take notes when God is teaching us.

If a busy housewife has to clear off a spot for Bible study during a crowded day, she is likely to put it off. But if she has a place where her Bible is always open and handy, whenever there is a lull in the storm she can grab a cup of coffee and sit down for a few minutes or more of pure refreshment and companionship.

Now, while working around the house, driving the car, ironing, shopping, or whatever I may be doing, some verse I have memorized will slip into my mind at an unexpected moment, and may be exactly the word I need.

When I regained consciousness after falling out of that tree in Mequon, I found I could not remember a single Bible verse. Suddenly I felt as a man must feel who learns the bank has failed and he has lost his life savings.

"Lord," I begged, "You can have anything I've got, but please give me back my Bible verses."

Out of nowhere came the words "I have loved thee with an everlasting love: therefore with lovingkindness have I drawn thee." I didn't even know where it was found. I do not recall ever memorizing it. But it was there, given back when I most needed it.

Collectibles

People are writing and talking about "collectibles." They can be a hedge against inflation, sort of a cushion in case of depression. They are small items that initially may have cost little or nothing but that increase startlingly in value in a relatively short period of time. Included are old stamps, rare coins, old photographs, paintings, even certain cans and bottles.

I got to thinking. What would be the best collectible for me? Something that would increase in value; something that would make me really wealthy; something I could share that would be a cushion in case of depression, and could provide comfort in case of the death of a loved one or old age.

I had it! Bible verses. I had started long ago.

In China, Miss Lucy Fletcher offered us, her students, $5.00 (a *lot* of money for a missionary's kid) if we would memorize the Sermon on the Mount. Hours and hours of going over and over Matthew 5, 6, 7. When the time came to recite it, I made one mistake so got only $4.50. But I wouldn't take one thousand times that amount in place of having memorized it.

The Reference Point

The State Highway Department in Pennsylvania once set out to build a bridge, working from both sides. When the workers reached the middle of the waterway, they found they were thirteen feet to one side of each other. Alfred Steinberg, writing some time ago in the *Saturday Evening Post*, went on to explain that each crew of workmen had used its own reference point.

There is a small bronze disk on the Meads' ranch in north central Kansas where the thirty-ninth parallel from the Atlantic to the Pacific crosses the ninety-eighth meridian from Canada to the Rio Grande.

The National Ocean Survey, a small federal agency whose business it is to locate the exact position of every point in the United States, uses the scientifically recognized reference point on the Meads' ranch. So far, no mistakes have been made, and none are expected.

All ocean liners and commercial planes come under the survey. The government can build no dams or even shoot off a missile without this agency to tell it exact locations— to the very inch.

"Location by approximation," the article goes on to say, "can be costly and dangerous."

The Reference Point for the Christian is the Bible. All values, judgments, and attitudes must be gauged in relationship to this Reference Point.

Grandparents are special.

Although we were deprived of our natural grandparents while growing up in China, the senior missionaries were like our own grandparents.

> Uncle Jimmie and Aunt Sophie Graham
> Dr. and Mrs. Woods
> Grandma and Grandpa Reynolds
> and others. . .

In the Orient which I knew, age was respected because it implied the accumulation of wisdom that the years bring. To have an old grandparent in the home was considered a privilege rather than a burden.

Once when Bill and I were in Tokyo on our way to the Korean crusade, we were taking a walk in the Imperial Gardens, which were open for the enjoyment of the public.

It was a hot Sunday afternoon, and a strong wind blew grit in our faces. Lots of families were out.

As we descended a steep incline from the upper garden, we heard a gale of merry laughter. Turning the corner, we met a whole family—the smiling grandmother in her wheelchair being pushed by her son (I assume), who was bent double with the effort, and behind the son the daughter-in-law (?), in turn pushing the son, surrounded by the rest of the family, all hugely enjoying the ridiculousness and fun of it. I wished for my mother so that we could push her around those lovely gardens in her wheelchair.

Our children did not get to see as much of Bill's parents as we would have liked. They lived in Charlotte. But the children were deeply influenced by their paternal grandparents because of their kindly and godly lives. Fortunately we lived much closer to my parents. Living across the road from them was one of the nicest things that ever happened to our first four children. (Ned was born after the move up the mountain.)

They were ideal grandparents: strict disciplinarians but full of love and fun.

Many nights the girls would spend with their grandparents. I can still see them, like three little stairsteps, dressed for bed and hugging their favorite blankets or pillows, as they climbed our curving drive and walked the short distance across the road to Daddy and Mother's.

Those evenings were always family times, as they had been in China. Games to be played, books to be read aloud. Mother made clothes for their dolls, nursed them when they were sick, let them help her work in her flowers in the spring and rake leaves in the fall and lick the pan after making a batch of fudge.

Since Daddy was a doctor, whenever medication or stitches were needed, he was available.

Both were great story tellers. They were happy Christians. They were part of God's special provision for us during the many occasions Bill was away on crusades. Just as Jesus promised, "He who leaves family for My sake and the Gospel's shall receive an hundredfold in this life" (see Mark 10:29, 30).

Those of you who have not had a loving Christian heritage can make sure your children have one. Even if you feel it is too late, commit the wasted years and lost opportunities to God. Love each one who comes to mind, and pray.

Then, look around for some young person you can encourage and help along the way.

Two Mrs. Grahams help Billy celebrate a birthday.
(Photo by Russ Busby.)

During his last year, Daddy served as Moderator of the Southern Presbyterian Church. Mother had had a stroke several years before which had left her confined to a wheelchair, with her speech slightly affected. Frequently, Daddy was up at four in the morning to have his Bible study and time of prayer so he could devote the rest of his day to Mother.

I stood by to help in any way I could, often taking the evening meal down to them and bringing Mother up to stay with me when Daddy would have to be gone for several days.

One morning when I dropped by to see how they were, I found Daddy on his knees in front of Mother, helping her put on her stockings.

Daddy had reached the point where he got up and down with difficulty. He, who had been an athlete in his younger days, and had always kept himself in top physical shape, now found himself with a painfully ulcerated toe that refused to heal due to the fact that he was a borderline diabetic and had lost circulation in his left leg.

He glanced up at me over his glasses, giving me his usual broad smile of welcome.

"You know," he said, returning to Mother's stocking, "these are the happiest days of our lives. Caring for your mother is the greatest privilege of my life."

And the nice thing was, he meant it.

The last year, when he had to make some trips as Moderator of the church, Mother would wait impatiently for his return. She knew the approximate time the plane would land and how long it would take him to drive from the airport. She would be the first to hear the wheels on the gravel in the driveway, the first to hear the car door slam and his quick step on the back porch.

If he was not fast enough to suit her, in her impatience she would give an imperious little cry that sounded more like "Nelsoo" than "Nelson." Or an impatient little hoot. In either case, his step would quicken.

Her dim eyes would be looking anxiously toward the dining room through which he must enter. Then he would be beside her, bending down to kiss her long and tenderly, coming up for air, and going down for seconds.

And all this after fifty-seven years of marriage.

And then, suddenly he was gone. When Mother woke up around 7:30 A.M. on August 2, 1973, she called Daddy to turn on the news. He was usually up by then, certainly prompt to respond.

But there was no answer. Then she knew that he was gone.

The doctor said he had died at dawn.

As Bill said, "It was about the time he usually got up."

And he did!

> "Nothing of God dies when a man of God dies."
> A. W. TOZER

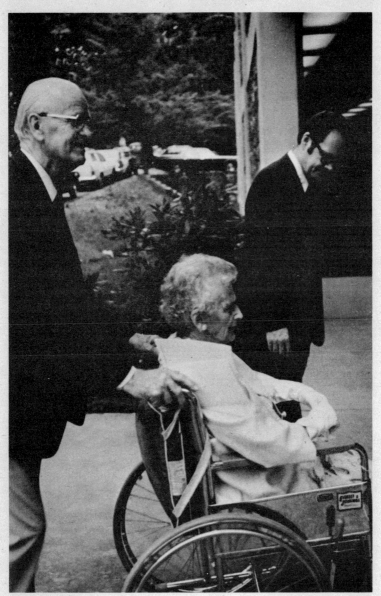

Dr. and Mrs. L. Nelson Bell, with Dr. Donald Mitchell. Ruth's father once told her, "Caring for your mother is the greatest privilege of my life." (Photo by Russ Busby.)

We felt that keeping Mother as happy as possible after Daddy died was more important than keeping her well.

We let her do exactly what she wanted, whether it was good for her or not.

I've seen too many old people whose lives were made miserable because of bossy children.

When she was ready, we moved her up to live with us. We had prepared the downstairs guest room years before with this in mind, putting in a bay window to add light. It had its own little fireplace and private bath.

But after a few weeks, we found that what Bill and I needed was what Mother did not need. We need quiet and privacy. Mother needed people.

When she asked if she could move back to her house, we said, "Whatever makes you happiest."

So we located a housekeeper and a companion and moved her back.

Friends and neighbors dropped in constantly. One day a group of students from the college came and gathered about her, sitting on whatever was available, spilling onto the floor. One had a guitar, and they sang hymns and choruses for her till the house bulged with music, and Mother knew she was surrounded by love.

Then she had a final stroke. I was in Mequon recovering from my fall when word reached us that Mother was in the hospital.

GiGi flew home with me. Rosa came, too, and Clayton from Dallas. We found Mother helpless and furious. Tubes were extending from everywhere. Her rings had been forcibly removed, and when the nurse tried to remove her partials as well, Mother, with her old spunk, snapped at her. Although she was unable to speak, I could read the anger and frustration in her eyes.

This might be a postponement of death for her, but it was certainly not a prolongation of life.

So I asked the doctor who had cared for her and Daddy for so long, if we could take her home. She might not live as long, but she would die happily.

"If all you children agree," he replied, "you have my permission."

Rosa rode in the ambulance with her. She said Mother looked worried till they passed through the arched stone Montreat Gate. Then her face lit up. In her slightly confused state, she may have thought we were taking her to a nursing home (a thing she dreaded).

It was a joy to see her settled comfortably in her own bed, in her loved and familiar surroundings.

Rosa was able to give her the necessary shots to keep her comfortable.

Mother, who all her life had loved music, who used to play the piano and sing like a bird, now asked only for "The King Is Coming."

Realizing that when a person is facing death and knows it, most music—even many hymns—have no appeal, we gathered a great pile of Christian records and marked every hymn that would speak to the dying. Taking them to our Christian radio station, we had them lift those particular hymns onto cassette tapes. Mother had a simple cassette recorder she was able to work, and she listened to those grand old hymns by the hour.

Then, quietly, on November 7, 1974, she joined Daddy.

It comes sooner or later to us all. All, that is, who have nests.

You have never seen a bird hanging onto her babies' tail feathers, with her beak herding them back into the nest when they would fly away. Quite the opposite. If the fledgling is reluctant, he is gently nudged out.

I had left Ned at a boarding school in England. The other children by now were either married or away in college. Bill was off on a crusade.

I dreaded returning to that now empty house.

But as I entered the front door and looked down the length of the hall and up the steps leading to the children's now vacant rooms, suddenly it wasn't empty. I was greeted by a living Presence, and I realized anew how true His last words were, "Lo, I am with you..." (Matthew 28:20). I was surrounded by loved memories and the comfortableness of knowing I was home. This was my base of operations.

Now the years ahead stretched vacant. What did God want me to do? Travel with Bill? I tried it for two years: two trips around the world, Manila, Hungary, Singapore, Poland, China, Europe. And I wound up a zombie. I cannot keep up with the man. In fact, taking me on a crusade is rather like a general taking his wife to battle with him. Our happiest times together are at home or on vacation (though he usually takes his vacations like the drivers of the Indianapolis 500 take their pit stops—as seldom and as quickly as possible).

So home is where I hope to stay for the most part. I hope to be here when any of the children or grandchildren need me. From my vantage point, I can look back on circumstances involving our children, situations I once felt were hopeless, only to see in disbelief and amazement as God brought order out of chaos, light out of darkness.

I will follow their struggles with peace in my heart. Battles may be lost, but God will win out in the end. We gave them to Him, each one uniquely loved, each as dear as the other: our most treasured possessions.

As each little family builds its nest, I shall be watching with interest and love, concern at times, but concern under-girded with confidence, knowing God is in control.

And I shall be enjoying Life!

Thomas Wolfe once wrote, "You can't go home again."

But we tried.

My two sisters, Rosa and Virginia, our brother Clayton, and I returned to our old home in China in May 1980.

I recalled those spiritual giants of my childhood. We visited Uncle Jimmy and Aunt Sophie's old house (now a wholesale grocery outlet), the girls' school where Lucy Fletcher had tutored us, the hospital compound (now an industrial school). So familiar, so changed. Our old home was graciously emptied for our inspection. Behind the welcoming banner stood all that was left—a pathetic reminder of the home that was—like an old woman, no longer loved or cared for.

We even located the Chinese house in which I was born.

For me it was like a death and a resurrection. Sentimental feelings for the place, nurtured lovingly over the decades, died. I realized afresh that God's work is not in buildings but in transformed lives.

Buildings fall into decay and eventually disappear. The transformed life goes on forever.

An unimpeachable source had informed me earlier that the Church in China today is both larger and stronger than when the missionaries left. The day of foreign missions as we have known them is a thing of the past. But God, who makes no mistakes, is in control. The Shepherd still cares for His sheep.

An old friend who heard of our coming and looked us up said, "The seed your father sowed is still bearing fruit. Most of the older Christians are dead, but the younger ones are carrying on."

"Please write a book," the girls urged.

"There are too many books already," I objected.

"But you've had a different sort of life..."

"And young mothers want to know how you managed..."

"Often, I didn't," I said.

"Say that, too. But you've learned from others."

I readily agreed.

"Okay. Let us learn from you."

"But we each have to learn in our own way. Things I learned or failed to learn, things that happened to me—all these might not fit another situation."

"But there are principles involved..."

"It wouldn't have to be an autobiography..."

"I should hope not!" I exclaimed.

"Okay. Will you start writing? Just start..."

So I started. That was two years ago. No, fifty. I can't remember when I wasn't scribbling something. Bits and pieces. I never finished a diary. I began every one optimistically on the first of January and flickered out shortly after. I think that is because some days are not worth writing about.

But I kept writing bits and pieces—things I didn't want to forget. It's rather like snapping pictures. You can capture something for keeps that would otherwise be forgotten tomorrow.

And that's a bit of what I've shared with you.

Prayer by a Bishop for the Members of His Church (Borrowed by This Mother for Her Children)

"Jesus, good Shepherd, they are not mine but yours,
for I am not mine but yours.
I am yours, Lord, and they are yours,
because by your wisdom you have created
both them and me,
and by your death you have redeemed us.
So we are yours, good Lord, we are yours,
whom you have made with such wisdom
and bought so dearly.
Then if you commend them to me, Lord,
you do not therefore desert me or them.
You commend them to me:
I commend myself and them to you.
Yours is the flock, Lord, and yours is the shepherd.
Be Shepherd of both your flock and shepherd.

"You have made an ignorant doctor [mother], a blind leader,
an erring ruler:
teach the doctor [mother] you have established,
guide the leader [mother] you have appointed,
govern the ruler that you have approved.
I beg you,
teach me what I am to teach,
lead me in the way that I am to lead,
rule me so that I may rule others.
Or rather, teach them, and me through them,
lead them, and me with them,
rule them, and me among them."

ANSELM, 1033-1109
Archbishop of Canterbury, 1093-1109
Translated by Sister Benedicta Ward, S.L.G.

P. S.

How I got myself into this I'll never quite know, but once in, there was no way out.

I wrote the first draft while I had the flu. The corrected manuscript returned, sounding just as if it had been written while I had the flu.

After a long line of interruptions, I caught the flu again. So while recuperating, I rewrote it. Back came the corrected manuscript—sounding exactly as though it had been written while recuperating from the flu.

Apologetically, knowing how even polite publishers feel about deadlines and publishing dates, I signed a contract for the first of August, and headed for Europe.

But the degenerative arthritis in my left hip (triggered seven years previously by "the fall") steadily worsened, making concentration difficult. Back in America, arrangements were made to proceed as soon as possible with a total hip replacement.

That meant a broken contract. I held my breath. But Victor Oliver, Revell's top editor, my inspiration and "cattle prod," sent word, "Forget the book. Just get well."

Once home again, pain free but exhausted, I called Victor.

"I think I have collected enough material," I said, "but I haven't the strength to put it together. Could you possibly send me a good editor to help me?"

"How about me?" came the humble reply.

That's how we got off the runway.

Today I want to thank Evelyn Freeland, my secetary, for so patiently typing and retyping pages and pages of material; I am grateful to my husband for calling a halt when he saw I couldn't go on; to Victor Oliver for graciously letting me off the hook when I couldn't continue, and for encouraging and helping me when I could; to Bill and Vivian Mead for sharing their lovely condominium with us for the final assault on the book.

These past two days, Victor has commandeered the dining-room table; Stephanie Wills (my husband's secretary) has set up her typewriter in the living room; I have stretched out on the couch; Bill Mead has returned to the States to earn enough to keep us all eating; Vivian has become a displaced person in her own apartment, retiring to her bedroom; and my Bill is a refugee on the beach!

The serenity of this spot has been shattered by the steady clatter of the typewriter, much shuffling of pages, continuous walking back and forth, arguments shouted against the noise of the waves on the beach, much laughter and many discussions, and the final settling for what we have here.

But a very special thanks to Maria Luisa, who kept us supplied with coffee and iced Manzanilla tea the whole two days —

Gracias!